Tan Lark Sye

Advocator and Founder of Nanyang University

Tan Lark Sye

Advocator and Founder of Nanyang University

Editors

Ong Chu Meng *(Nanyang University Alumnus, Singapore)*
Lim Hoon Yong *(Nanyang University Alumnus, Singapore)*
Ng Lai Yang *(Independent Scholar)*

 **World Scientific**

**Nanyang University Alumni
Association of Hong Kong**

Published by

World Scientific Publishing Co. Pte. Ltd.

5 Toh Tuck Link, Singapore 596224

USA office: 27 Warren Street, Suite 401-402, Hackensack, NJ 07601

UK office: 57 Shelton Street, Covent Garden, London WC2H 9HE

Library of Congress Cataloging-in-Publication Data
Tan Lark Sye : advocator and founder of Nanyang University / edited by Ong Chu Meng,
Lim Hoon Yong, Ng Lai Yang.
     pages cm
   ISBN 978-9814641494 -- ISBN 978-9814644754 (pbk)
   1. Tan, Lark Sye, 1897–1972. 2. Educators--Singapore--Biography 3. Philanthropists--
Singapore--Biography. 4. Nanyang University--History. 5. Education, Higher--Singapore--History.
I. Ong, Chu Meng, editor of compilation.
   LA2383.S552T367 2015
   378.5957--dc23
                              2014043942

British Library Cataloguing-in-Publication Data
A catalogue record for this book is available from the British Library.

In-house Editor: Dong Lixi

Typeset by Stallion Press
Email: enquiries@stallionpress.com

Printed in Singapore

Dedication by Tan Lark Sye's Family

December 1997

It has been 25 years since our forebear, Mr. Tan Lark Sye left us. Even today, upon the 100th anniversary of his birth, there are still friends who would go through the arduous task of publishing this commemorative anthology. We, his children and grandchildren, are comforted by such warmth that still remains in this world.

Our forebear spared no efforts in his selfless devotion to humanity, his career, his fellow clansmen, the entire Chinese race and our nation. In addition, we are filled with pride and admiration for his dauntless spirit in the establishment of Nanyang University in the face of adverse circumstances and difficulties.

As his descendants, our achievements are incomparable to his monumental achievements. For this, we are ashamed of ourselves. Yet, we sincerely hope that the Nantah spirit that he stirred up will be passed on for perpetuity in this part of the world and shine forth with ever-increasing brilliance.

We would like to express our sincere gratitude to all the individuals and social groups for their concerted endeavour to give birth to this book successfully.

南洋大學倡辦人
陳六使先生百年誕

飲 水 思 源

潘受

For the 100th birth anniversary of Tan Lark Sye – advocator and
founder of Nanyang University:

When drinking water, think of the source

Inscribed by Pan Shou   Dated: December 1997

Portrait of Tan Lark Sye (1897–1972), advocator and founder of Nanyang University.

Contents

Preface

Lim Hoon Yong
Editor

The collection of essays published in 1997 by the Nantah Alumni in commemoration of the centenary of its founder, the late Mr. Tan Lark Sye, will soon be made available in English. I have the honour to be invited to write a preface for its publication.

In the words of its chief editor, this English version is aimed at enabling non-Chinese educated readers to better understand the background in establishing the Nanyang University in mid-1950s; the Odyssey like journey it has undertaken in its two decades of operation until its eventual shut down in 1980.

However, in retrospective, the founding of Nanyang University needs to be viewed and re-evaluated in a historical perspective. It is most significant because it opened the floodgates for university education to be made available to a greater number of eligible students irrespective of languages and school backgrounds. University was no longer seen and regarded as the "ivory tower".

It is also significant because during the period when it was under review, colonial legacy prejudicing against Chinese school turnouts for admission to local university was still prevailing. If not for the Nanyang University, hundreds of Nantah Alumni including the writer would not have been able to receive tertiary education in those days. The many talents of graduates who had advanced themselves in overseas institutions and engaged in scientific and academic researches would have been lost.

Equally significant, Nantah was the first University to adopt a "credits system" in lieu of the "academic year system" in all its courses of study. This augured well for the University of Singapore and Nanyang Technological University to later on convert to the credits system in most of their courses of study.

However, notwithstanding the shutdown of the University in 1980, its establishment and eventual closure still remain an issue of concern for those who invariably contributed to its founding i.e. its alumni and the communities that participated enthusiastically in its funding programmes. But, for now, join me to pay tribute to the founder of our Alma Mater, for without him and his commitment, the founding of Nanyang University would not have been possible.

On this note I pray for him to rest in peace.

Acknowledgments

This collection of essays is based on a Chinese book published in 1997, on the occasion of Mr Tan Lark Sye's centenary birthday. The first group of the organisations and people we ought to thank are those who made the 1997 publication possible. Without that Chinese publication, this English edition would not have come into being.

For this English edition, we must thank the organisations and those who planned the publication, various editors, authors and proof readers, and those who remained invisible but contributed significantly. In particular, let us mention the Tan Lark Sye family, Nanyang University Alumni Association of Hong Kong, World Scientific Publishing Co Pte Ltd, Pan Shou (Pan Kuo Chu), Lim Soon Tiong, Phua Kok Khoo, Ong Chu Meng, Lim Hoon Yong, Ng Lai Yang, Choi Kwai Keong, Koay How Khim, Lim How Seng, Au Yue Pak, Ng Kim Eng, Tan Yam Seng, He Hua, Jimmy Low, Dong Lixi, Yam Siew Khim, Gan Kok Koon, Wei Yu Hui, Leck Kim Koon and Siw Ming Mei.

Chapter 1

Sparkle of a Glorious Feat in S.E. Asian Chinese

Ong Chu Meng
Chief Editor

Armed with his extraordinary intrepidity, Mr. Tan Lark Sye volunteered for the epochal mission to lead the momentous movement to establish Nanyang University and turn it into a fortress of Chinese education of the highest standards. Nanyang University has produced countless talents as academics and professionals, and perhaps more importantly, a spirit of perseverance, altruism, and camaraderie, fondly called the Nantah Spirit.

The founder passed away on September 17, 1972. Teachers and students of the University draped the University flag over his coffin to pay him their last respects amidst the attendance of thousands of members of the public during the funeral procession. Our memories are so vivid that the ceremony seems to have happened only yesterday. The University flag over Mr. Tan's coffin was embossed with the University logo of three circles in yellow, blue and red. Yellow was symbolic of China's legendary ruler the Huang Di, and the yellow star on the banner implied Nanyang University's mission to propagate the Chinese culture. The three interlocking circles were symbolic of the three main ethnic groups (Chinese, Malays, and Indians) coexisting and interacting with one another peacefully. The flag presented by the teachers and students of the University showed their highest respects to the founder on his demise. The flag also reminded us of the founder's teachings to us:

1

that Chinese culture and Chinese education ought to be treasured and passed on and that the ethnic groups ought to coexist and engage among themselves in cultural dialogues.

R.I.P. dear Mr. Tan, we will not disappoint you.

Mr. Tan's life is a cross section of our forefathers who variegated their difficult business enterprises. He witnessed and participated in the history of his century.

Orphaned at a young age, Mr. Tan had only a few years of formal education. He came to S.E. Asia at the age of 19, but he was exceptionally industrious and enterprising. In only a few years, he managed to set up his own business and became a magnate in the rubber plantation business.

In the colonial era, both the people and businesses were oppressed. Mr. Tan, together with Mr. Lee Kong Chian, tried to break the Western powers' monopoly on the rubber trade, and shift the trade centres from consumers' New York and London to producers' Kuala Lumpur and Singapore. Mr. Tan pointed out: "Western traders have all along plotted to deprive the Chinese merchants in Malaya and Singapore of their legitimate claim to be the primary wholesalers of rubber. In 1953, that is before I became the chairman of the Rubber Traders Association, the Westerntraders pressurised the government to set up a rubber export regulatory board, whose purpose was to benefit the Western merchants at the expense of the locals. The latter paid hundreds of thousands of dollars to fund the board which only works for Western traders. Confronted with this betrayal, I have no choice but to struggle, boldly."

Mr. Tan also expressed his disgust with governmental measures to restrict trade. He said, "After WW2, neo-colonialism reared its ugly head in the guise of food control, currency control, and economic aid to undeveloped countries. These measures in fact hinder the economic developments, and the people naturally continue to live in poverty."

After experiencing both British and Japanese colonial rule, Mr. Tan felt that people without political rights were very miserable, and compared them to meat on a chopping block, where the alien rulers were the butchers, wielding their cleavers.

Before WW2, most overseas Chinese regarded themselves as temporary residents whose homeland was China, and actively participated in China's War of Resistance against the Japanese. After the war, their attitude began to change, and they increasingly identified themselves with the country they lived in. Mr. Tan was one of the leaders who swiftly and bravely adopted this new attitude.

In 1951, as the president of the Chinese Chamber of Commerce, he regularly led the Chinese to demand citizenship and rights to participate in politics. He said, "Previously we did not engage in politics. Now times have changed, it has become impossible for us not to participate in politics."

In 1955, he led the Chamber of Commerce to demand for Chinese right to citizenship, the right to participate in politics, and Chinese language to be made one of the four official languages. He said, "As the Chamber of Commerce is the premier Chinese society, it cannot disregard its duty to lead the Chinese community to press for its rights. Making sacrifices are much better than leaving behind despised names. If one day the Chinese here were expelled en masse, the cause would definitely be our inaction today."

Mr. Tan's most outstanding achievement is his founding of Nanyang University. In the fifties, the political climate underwent a big change, mainly due to the establishment of the Communist Government in China. Chinese culture and education in Singapore were severely suppressed. The Chinese-educated students had no opportunity of university education. Mr. Tan started a mass-participating movement to establish the Nanyang University. Almost every sector of the Chinese community responded with great enthusiasm.

In addition of his personal donation of five million dollars, he also persuaded the Hokkien Association to donate five hundred acres of land for the university site. In the process, he refuted and defeated arguments against the establishment of the university. He was personally involved in every aspect of the setting up of the university, like the way he handled the case of Lin Yutang. Eventually he managed to raise the status of the University.

Mr. Tan also fought relentlessly for Nanyang University's degrees to be recognised (by the government). Under his leadership, Chinese education in S.E. Asia became readily available from primary level to university.

On April 2, 1960 and March 3, 1961, Mr. Tan said at the graduation ceremonies: "The reputation of Nanyang University is the sum of the reputations of all its graduates. What does the University expect from you in return? Only two things: first, your loyalty to your country, and second, that you work for the maximum welfare of the greatest numbers of your fellow citizens." He added: "Serve the people. Be honest, be brave, be humble, and forever industrious in achieving academic excellence."

Nanyang University went on to nurture tens of thousands of graduates who, like the seeds of a dandelion, spread across Singapore, Malaysia, and beyond. Wherever they were, they rooted, blossomed and bore fruits. They served in every sector of commerce and industry. However, the most valuable contribution lay in the grooming of thousands of devoted teachers and educators who helped promote the Chinese culture.

December 20, 1997 marked the hundredth birthday of Mr. Tan, and on this day alumni of Nanyang University around the world gathered in Hong Kong, to commemorate Mr. Tan's 100th birthday. The theme of commemoration was "when drinking water, think of the source." It was also an occasion to remind the alumni that they should never cease to emulate Mr. Tan's example of patriotism and sacrifice for national culture.

Mr. Tan has left us for 25 years. Some commentators thought an apt description of his legacies would be the following poem:

> Thunderous drums liven up the Zhao Village,
> A blind storyteller takes his stage;
> They all love titillating tales: who cares
> How folklore besmirched Cai Yong the sage?

Mr. Tan Lark Sye's life remained a tale to be cherished and retold for generations.

Mr. Tan lived in a transitional period of great turbulence in his lifetime. He felt deeply committed to face challenges for the good for his people. He impressed on people as a man of vision; a leader of exceptional character. His deeds and undeterred spirit must be highlighted in history for the sake of our posterity.

Mr. Tan made valuable contribution in finance and energy to the endeavour of culture and education out of his belief that "it is better to bequeath skills to our young rather than leaving money behind for them because without specialised skill, one would find it difficult to eke out a living in modern society least to say to build his career." He further illustrated: "Money gain and loss is just like the rise and fall of tide. During high tide you channel it for irrigating farmland and you can expect a good harvest in return. However if you do not harness benefits of the rising tide, it would soon recede. Likewise those with children who have passion in learning why not facilitate them in learning? Those with money and believe in the philosophy of high tide–low tide, why not wisely use your money to benefit the community?"

For the sake of culture and education for the future generations, his noble character and his generosity drove him to found Nanyang University which in turn was instrumental in laying excellent gene of the Chinese culture for our progeny.

Tan Lark Sye is figured like gold hidden in ore and diamond in the rough. When the tides of time polished off the crust and sand, that gold, that diamond will sparkle splendidly and brilliantly in the long river of history.

The grand funeral procession in drizzle; the flag draped on the coffin; the awesome sense of mourning among hundreds of thousands in attendance, his kind teaching in whisper and his earnest hope and inspirations 25 years ago seemed to have taken place just only yesterday. The eternal image of this historical giant present itself before us time and again.

Chapter 2

Mr. Tan Lark Sye — Founder of Nanyang University

Dictated by Pan Shou, and transcribed by his son Dr. Pan Siying

On a Saturday in September 1972, Mr. Su Jun Zhu came to my house and said, "Lao Liu is resigning his position as chairman of the Hokkien Association. We all disagreed with his decision, but he seemed determined. He also said he had not seen you for years. Would you come to our dinner tomorrow evening at the Tanjong Rhu Singapore Club?"

I accepted his invitation.

The next evening, Jun Zhu fetched me to Tanjong Rhu Club. The club seemed more deserted than before. The first to welcome us was Ang Chye Chuan, leaning on his walking stick. Not far behind him was Tan Lark Sye, also with a walking stick.

Lark Sye explained that he felt all right, except that his legs seemed weak, hindering his walking. I advised him to rest more. He knew that I preferred food from Chui Huai Lim, so he ordered some dishes from that restaurant. I remembered those who were seated with us included Quek Bok Song and Ng Tai Chun. Lark Sye's favourite dish was shark's fin, so he would usually finish off the rest of this dish after all of us had been served. It was no exception that night, and he even shared with me half of his portion of the shark's fin.

I took my leave at 10 p.m. Lark Sye saw me off personally at the main entrance, extending to me the same formality as he would usually treat new guests.

Early next morning, Ng Aik Huan told me by telephone that Brother Lark Sye had passed away, and said he would come to fetch me and go to Lark Sye's home together.

I told Aik Huan that it was really hard to believe: "How can it be! We had dinner together just last evening, but you weren't there. Maybe you heard wrongly." Stunned by the sudden news, I wondered: "Had the dinner last evening turned out to be our farewell dinner for Lark Sye?"

Aik Huan replied emphatically, "It was his wife Mrs. Tan Lark Sye who broke the sad news to me personally. I'm coming over to pick you up right away."

When we arrived at Lark Sye's house in Katong, he was already laid to rest in a brown coffin with golden handle rings and placed in the sombre mourning hall. Aik Huan and I bowed and paid our last respects to our dear friend.

His family told me that he would usually walk round the garden whenever he came back home but, last evening he made an exception. He complained about chest pain and walked straight to his room upstairs.

We immediately formed a funeral committee, and I wrote a eulogy couplet, as follows:

"Success in Enterprise, Sacrifice to Education: Glory in Life, No Regrets in Death.
Resolute by Nature, Honest since Young: Deeds often Misunderstood, Fame lives on."

Staff and students from the Nanyang University also came to me for an inscription for their joint obituary, and I wrote: *"Source of the Spring: Root of the Tree."*

Countless friends and relatives came to mourn him, despite the size of his house.

I got to know Tan Lark Sye after knowing Mr. Tan Kah Kee and Mr. Lee Kong Chian. I came back to Singapore from war-ravaged China together with my family at the end of WW2 in 1949. I first met Lark Sye on a Saturday evening when I was dining at Ee Hoe Hean Club. Later we often kept in touch and he graciously invited me to the Club several times. In those turbulent days, the anti-British colonialism sentiment among Singapore people was very intense, and seemed capable of exploding any time.

In 1953, I was present at the evening function of the Hokkien Association held at the Ee Hoe Hean Club. At this function, Mr. Tan spoke of his dream of setting up a Chinese-language university.

He said: "Until now, Chinese high school graduates in Singapore and Malaya can only go to China for further studies. Since our government does not recognise the New China, students who go to China will not be allowed to return. Without a local university, there will not be a complete education system. In the future we will be short of Chinese teachers, and that will threaten the existence of even primary schools. We will be faced with a future without qualified successors of the Chinese heritage. If you are agreeable with this, I will donate five million dollars to fund this proposal."

Five million dollars was a huge sum in those days, and that was also the biggest donation received for the University.

With applause from all who were present, his proposal was passed unanimously, and so began the story of Nanyang University.

I remembered that towards the end of WW2, the Atlantic Charter declared, "... with the end of the War, colonial rule shall be abolished and the peoples in the colonies shall be entitled to enjoy the rights of self-governance and independence, freedom of religious beliefs and education policies. No country is allowed to interfere in any other country's internal state affairs, and in particular, education in the native language shall be respected."

The British colonialists were stirring up racial conflicts everywhere to facilitate their divide and rule strategy. So the government would surely not approve the setting up of a Chinese-language university. A fierce debate ensued, involving a wide spectrum of influential people, including Malcolm MacDonald, then the British Commissioner-General for S.E. Asia, Tan Cheng Lock, a well-known lawyer from Malacca, and David Marshall, a famous Jewish lawyer in Singapore, who paid a thousand dollars as membership fee to join the Nanyang University. In the late 1940s and 1950s, the struggle between the colonialists and local people erupted and intensified.

In campaigning for Nanyang University, Mr. Tan once described material wealth as being like the rising and receding tide. "When the tide rises, channel it for irrigation and to nourish the farmland, and it will reward you with rich gains. But hurry, because it will soon recede. Similarly, why not help the poor students study while you are still capable of doing so?"

Like a deafening thunder, Lark Sye's appeal to establish Nanyang University awakened all walks of life in Singapore and Malaya. The British rulers were startled by these developments and tried to hinder the movement. But the entire Chinese community responded to the appeal passionately and selflessly. Fund raising through tickets sales of concerts, contests, taxi and trishaw rides were donated to the University.

There were also many who remained behind the scene, including anonymous supporters. A better-known contributor was Teng Mah Seng, Chairman of the Siong Leng Musical Association and a rubber trader.

One major contributor was the Lee Foundation, whose founder Mr. Lee Kong Chian pledged to contribute the equivalent of 10% of all contributions received during the period 1953–1957. He also promised scholarships for poor Singaporean students wanting to study in the University. Later, when the Singapore government agreed to assume responsibility for these scholarships, the Lee Foundation re-directed the funds to support impoverished Malayan applicants to the University.

Then, a very unpleasant incident happened, later commonly known as the Lin Yu Tang incident. This caused some setback for the smooth developments of the University. But the eventual settlement of the incident also exposed the resoluteness and dynamism of Tan Lark Sye.

When he found out President of the University Lin Yu Tang's expensive budget and design aimed for a First Class University, he thought Lin was ignorant and ridiculous. He decided to make immediate painful sacrifice to save his original plan, much like doctors performing amputations to save life.

It was a Saturday evening in February 1955, when Ng Aik Huan called me, saying "Lark Sye has a very serious disagreement with Lin Yu Tang. You have to come over."

I went to the appointed place, a small air-conditioned room in Ee Hoe Hean building. Soon Tan Lark Sye came, together with Kuah Chin Lai and Ng Aik Huan.

Lark Sye said, "You must have heard something about this matter over the grapevine. What should we do now?"

I replied, quite bluntly, that Nanyang University was a matter of concern for the entire society of Singapore and Malaya, and that we ought to make public Lin's plan and budget, so that the matter could be resolved by mass discussions.

Lark Sye smiled, and said, "Let's go for dinner."

The next morning Lark Sye personally invited reporters from all the local papers and handed them copies of the complete set of Dr. Lin's reports and budget, for public release.

The following day, which was a Monday, the reports in the newspapers stirred up a public uproar in Singapore and Malaya. Before long, even the New York-based United Daily also labelled Lin Yu Tang as as a "buffoon disguising as gentle lady." Soon after, Lin and his chosen staff all collected their severance pay and left.

On March 15, 1956, Nanyang University held its Opening Ceremony, which was simple but solemn. The interlinked tri-colour flag fluttered proudly in the wind, telling the whole world that the Mission had been accomplished!

Today, 41 years later, when we recall the past — despite the biased British colonial rule in the 1950s, the enforcement of the Emergency Act, the various elements of instability in Singapore and Malaya — it is not far from the truth when I say that Nanyang University would not have existed without Tan Lark Sye. Righteous and outspoken, regardless of any risk to his reputation, Lark Sye sounded the call and the populace responded resoundingly. Thus was the most glorious chapter in the history of Chinese education in Singapore and Malaya, Mr. Tan's finest hour.

Chapter 3

Tan Lark Sye and the Evolution of His National Identity

Choi Kwai Keong

Tan Lark Sye (1897–1972) is a famous man widely known in Singapore and Malaya. He was a native of Jimei Town, Tong'An County, Fujian Province, which was also the birthplace of Tan Kah Kee. The latter had great influence over Lark Sye. Lark Sye in particular admired Tan Kah Kee's moral edifice and patriotism. Lark Sye built his business from scratch, and his Aik Hoe Rubber Company soon became one of the kingpins of rubber trade in Singapore and Malaya. He was the president of the Chinese Chamber of Commerce and Hokkien Association for many years. In 1953, he led the campaign to set up Nanyang University, which was enthusiastically supported by all Chinese in S.E. Asia.

This chapter attempts to analyse Tan Lark Sye's remarkable transformation of national identity: from a Chinese nationalist to a patriotic Singaporean.

National Identity Before WW2

Before WW2, among the Chinese in Singapore, only Straits-born Chinese and a few of the rich and powerful could gain the legal status of a British Subject, with the rest being treated as foreigners residing in Singapore. Tan Lark Sye (born in China) was therefore a non-British Subject, and he naturally regarded himself as a Chinese citizen.

In the 1930s, the Japanese imperialists intensified its invasion of China, beginning with the 9/18 Incident (Mukden or Shenyang Incident) in 1931 and the 1/28 Incident (Shanghai Incident) in 1932. These calamities in China roused an unprecedented upsurge of Chinese patriotism among the Chinese in Singapore and Malaya, leading to a series of fund-raising and boycotts of Japanese goods. The anti-Japanese sentiment reached a new peak after the Lugouqiao (Marco Polo Bridge) Incident on 7/7 of 1937. Led by Tan Kah Kee, every Chinese, regardless of social status, contributed to the war efforts in China. Urged by Tan Kah Kee, some young mechanics even went to Yunnan of China to help construct the Yunnan–Burma Highway. There weren't any doubts that Tan Lark Sye was among the anti-Japan zealots.

Tan Lark Sye's concern for China was well reflected in his stated wishes on the 30th anniversary of the founding of the Republic of China (in or around 1941):

(1) "May our motherland have a wise and incorrupt government. Take my home province Fujian for instance, people are very unhappy with the provincial government led by Chen Yi. If corruption is not brought under control, how can China progress?"
(2) "May our motherland be united. I have the very disturbing news that the Nationalists and the Communists are on the verge of warring again. Thankfully, the tension has been properly defused by the Central government. National unity must prevail if we want to resist foreign aggression."
(3) "May our motherland persevere in resisting foreign aggression, for there is no alternative."

Tan repeatedly referred to China as motherland, clearly revealing how he identified himself with China then.

Still Concerned With China Immediately After WW2

After the end of WW2, civil war immediately broke out between the Communists and Nationalists in China. This caused the Chinese community to split into two camps, pro-Communist and pro-Nationalist. Tan Kah Kee and the leaders of Chinese Democratic League supported the Chinese Communist Party to oppose Chiang Kai Shek's Nationalist Party (Kuomintang). On the other hand, some conservative Kuomintang Party members, who opposed the Chinese Communist Party, gained control of some key provincial associations and Chinese-medium schools. The highest representative institution of the Chinese community, the Chinese Chamber of Commerce, was also split by the conflict. The Chamber was splintered into three factions: left, right, and neutral. However, the Hokkien Association became Tan Kah Kee's political stronghold. As a key executive member of both the Chamber and the Hokkien Association, Tan Lark Sye made his position abundantly clear that he supported Tan Kah Kee's inclinations.

By early 1949, the outcome of the civil war in China was clearly in favour of the Communists. In his exhilaration, Tan Kah Kee returned to China on May 5 that year to see the new China, and to explore the possibility of participating in its new development. Over the next few years, Tan Lark Sye took over as the Chairman of the Hokkien Association.

With Tan Lark Sye at the helm, Hokkien Association continued to be actively supportive of Tan Kah Kee and New China. In May 1949 (before liberation of Fujian Province) the executive committee of the Association held an emergency meeting of all Association members to pass a resolution to support Tan Kah Kee's appeal (from Hong Kong) to all military and administrative institutions, civil organisations and the people of Fujian to rise in support of Tan Kah Kee's call to save the province and its people. The appeal also urged the people to welcome liberation and safeguard economic and cultural establishments. The remaining Kuomintang military and administrative personnel were urged to accept liberation, stop futile resistance, and stop destruction.

On October 10 (Double Ten Festival), a few days after the founding of New China (on October 1, 1949) the Hokkien Association brought together all the staff and students from its four affiliated schools for a convention to commemorate the founding of Republic of China (中华民国). Tan Lark Sye made a speech, in which he strongly denounced the ousted Kuomintang regime, and welcomed the new government in Beijing. The convention resolved to telegraph Chairman Mao Zedong to congratulate him.

The above account showed that Tan Lark Sye was still politically inclined towards China.

Realignment of National Identity in the Fifties

Having been elected as chairman of the Chinese Chamber of Commerce between 1950 and 1952, Tan Lark Sye showed a subtle shift of his political inclinations away from China towards Singapore. It eventually reached the stage where Tan called on Singaporean Chinese to be more aware and concerned with local politics. He even reminded the local Chinese that they were Singaporeans.

The following factors may have caused his shift of political stand:

(1) Since the foundation of the Aik Hoe Rubber Company in 1924, the Tan brothers worked hard and built up a strong bastion. This enabled it to survive the Great Depression well. The company resumed its business after WW2, and when the Korean War broke out in 1950, the company reaped huge profits as the price of rubber rocketed. Tan Lark Sye became a rubber magnate and an influential industrial and commercial captain. Comfortable environment naturally made him accept Singapore as home.

(2) In the early 1950s, Britain had to adjust its colonial policies because of new geopolitical realities. A self-governed and subsequently independent Singapore seemed inevitable. It made good political and economic sense for the Chinese to choose to remain in Singapore, instead of returning to China. In the several years before and after 1950, some parochial nationalists voiced radical views to cast doubt on the loyalty of the Chinese. Tan made a timely realignment of his political affiliation and encouraged the local Chinese to regard themselves as Singaporeans whose first duty was loyalty to Singapore, and whose inalienable right was citizenship of Singapore.

Striving for Citizenship for Chinese in Singapore

As Chairman of the Chamber of Commerce, Tan actively campaigned for mass citizenship. At the end of February 1951, the Chamber submitted a memorandum to the Colonial Governor, petitioning for the relaxation of citizenship criteria, to enable the more than 220,000 Chinese residents (who had been living in Singapore for many years) to acquire citizenship. But the Governor made no response.

Before WW2, all the legislators of Singapore were officially appointed. After the war, a general election of the legislative assembly was held for the first time in March 1948. The legislature was not representative, and only those who were British subjects were eligible for voting. Thus, Chinese immigrants, who made up the vast majority of adult Chinese, were not eligible to vote, while the eligible Chinese were somewhat indifferent. By 1951, when the number of elected legislators was increased to nine, the Chinese voters remained indifferent to local politics.

This phenomenon deeply disturbed Tan Lark Sye. At the overseas Chinese conference on May 11, 1951, he addressed the conference as its chairman, and said, "In the past, overseas Chinese were indifferent to local politics, but now times had changed. Similarly, in the past the Chamber never dabbled in local politics, but since it had to change. The chamber ought to be concerned with politics and the Chinese people ought to fight for voting rights for the legislature and the City Council. They should organise themselves and help the less well-informed to register for citizenship, and try to get those who care for the well-being of the Chinese elected as legislators."

At the beginning of March 1952, before he relinquished his office as the Chairman of the Chinese Chamber of Commerce, Tan said, "After WW2, the British repeatedly promised the eventual independence for Malaya. Henthforth, the Chinese Chamber of Commerce would lead the Chinese in striving for seats in the legislative and municipal councils." He also appealed to all those Chinese eligible for voting to register themselves as voters. Otherwise, he said, the overseas Chinese would encounter numerous difficulties and uncertainties in doing business. He also urged the Chinese to unite to preserve their deserved place in Singapore, which they should now regard as home.

Thereafter, the Chamber pressed very hard for Chinese citizenship rights, and met on many occasions the Governor, Colonial Office bureaucrats, and the Linde Constitution Committee members. Tan Lark Sye took part in all these meetings.

Appeal to Voters: Use Your Votes

In early 1953, the Linde Constitution Committee started work on reviewing the constitution of Singapore. After three months the committee published its findings, which proposed the setting up of a 32-seat legislative council, comprising 25 elected members, four appointed members, and three ex-officio members. With the increased number of elected members, registered voters now had a larger participation of politics.

The Chamber of Commerce set up a Committee to encourage Chinese voters, who numbered more than 200,000, to exercise their voting rights in order to protect their rights and welfare.

In every electoral ward, the Chamber organised election rallies, complemented with Lion Dance, Chinese martial arts and music. On January 15, 1955, more than 10,000 people turned up at the rally held in the Tanjong Pagar district, in which Tan spoke and declared passionately that the local Chinese had now chosen Singapore as their homeland. He also urged the Chinese to be more politically aware, participate more actively in state affairs, and to vote wisely. He also listed some unreasonable measures taken by the post-war government, which could be rectified if voters chose their representatives wisely.

Concern that Some Citizenship Issues Still Remained

Tan was frustrated that the citizenship issue continued to be unresolved. In April 1956, Mr. David Saul Marshall, the first Chief

Minister of Singapore, led his Merdeka (meaning "independence" in Malay) delegation to London to negotiate with the British on self-rule and independence. The Chinese Chamber of Commerce requested Marshall to bring up the issue of citizenship for Chinese. On this issue Tan made a speech at a banquet at the Tanjong Rhu Club. He said that the Chinese had migrated to Singapore a long time ago, and should now be treated as natives. He urged the Chinese to fight for citizenship fearlessly, or risk being blamed by their descendants for dodging this sacred duty thrust upon them by history. He encouraged the Chinese to enlist their children in the army and police. Equitable participation in the uniformed services was a pre-requisite for the protection of civil rights. He also believed that it had been unwise of most Chinese to avert the government's implementation of the Public Service Act.

Tan urged all Singaporeans to regard themselves as "Singaporeans first", and relegate ethnic identity to the back burner. At the sending-off banquet held in honour of the Sino–Japanese Trade delegation, he introduced himself as a permanent resident of Singapore. He again talked about citizenship issue, and lamented Marshall's seeming lack of direction and decisiveness on this issue. After stepping down as Chief Minister, Marshall accompanied a delegation to China, purportedly to discuss the issue of dual nationality of Singaporean Chinese. Tan reminded him that he had not been authorised to act on behalf of Singaporean Chinese, and that the citizenship issue did not involve a third party which Beijing was. Finally, he reminded the delegation that Singaporeans should not be categorised into ethnic groups.

A Flexible and Frank Person

Tan Lark Sye had only a few years of formal eduction. Upon arrival in Singapore as a young man, he began his career by working at Tan Kah Kee's Khiam Aik (Qian Yi) Company. Soon he amassed enough capital and trade knowledge to set up his own Aik Hoe Company. After many years of hard work he became a magnate in the rubber trade. The experience he gained from the rubber trade made him astute, responsive, nimble and decisive. More importantly, he acquired the rare quality of political acumen. He realised that without political muscle, all economic gains could be easily taken away. He therefore urged people to be politically aware and united. He could be blunt, at times even brash, in criticising the government and politicians. Many appreciated these attributes in him, but some were offended.

At midnight of September 10, 1972, Tan suffered a heart attack and was rushed to hospital. But he passed away the next day, aged 76.

How hath the Meteor fallen!

Chapter 4

Tan Lark Sye's Passion for Universal Education

In Memory of the 100th Anniversary of His Birthday

Koay How Khim

A Divine Book Without Words

A copy of a very special posthumous honours record, *Commemorative Volume for the 1st Anniversary of Mr. Tan Lark Sye's Demise,* published in 1973, is laid before me. I suddenly feel inexplicable numbness and melancholy. The physique of the book is so disproportionate to the deserved stature of the man who is the subject of the book. The book has 12 pages, comprising Mr. Tan's portrait, a photo of the commemorative bronze statue, photos of the funeral procession, photos of the ground-breaking ceremony for the construction of Nanyang University, and some eulogistic writings by the funeral organising committee and members of the public. The excellent paper quality and binding cannot make up for the deficiency of this book.

   Some may compare this book favourably with the Chinese mythical Heavenly (or Divine) Book Without Words. Apart from the elegiac couplets that provided a much condensed overview of Tan's life, such as "A successful entrepreneur and a great benefactor to education" and "his deeds are praiseworthy and his good reputation lives on", the book has no other accounts of his life. Considering Tan's revered position in the Chinese society, such lack of biographical details seems deliberate, is puzzling and eerie.

To put things in perspective, the turbulent 1960s were recent and vivid in 1973 when the book was published. Memories of racial riots and ideological conflicts still affected people's everyday life. Although he did not participate actively in party politics, Tan was nonetheless dragged into the furore because some saw him as favouring some Nanyang University graduates who stood for elections. In such circumstances, it was already a miracle that Mr. Tan's posthumous honours record was published without undue third-party interference.

Today, almost 40 years later, the turbulence of those momentous years has largely subsided. It may be pertinent for us to review Tan Lark Sye's life, analyse his merits and demerits, successes and failures, and rights and wrongs, upon the centennial anniversary of his birth this year. Our efforts will be well spent if we can reposition him to the right place in history.

Half a Century of Entrepreneurship

In 1916, at the age of 19, Tan left his poverty-stricken home village in China and migrated to Singapore. In 1923, after years of hard work at Tan Kah Kee's enterprises, Tan Lark Sye and his elder brother Boon Kak started a rubber shop — Lian Hoe Rubber Shop — which was incorporated as Aik Hoe Rubber Company a year later. It was also involved in the business of smoked rubber sheet. From then on, he never looked back.[1]

During the Great Depression in the 1930s, businesses around the world withered, bringing down many established rubber merchants and plantation owners. But Tan, with his exceptional business acumen and audacity, turned adversities into opportunities. By 1938, Aik Hoe already established itself as a leading rubber trade player, with business interests in almost the entire S.E Asia. It also had agencies in New York and London to facilitate sales to the Western world.

As the WW2 ended, Aik Hoe was resurrected after a hiatus in the war years. However, due to the British military administration's control of the rubber trade, Aik Hoe made little progress, until 1947 when free trade was restored. When the Korean War broke out in 1950, rubber became much sought-after and its price rocketed. The shrewd Mr. Tan quickly seized this opportunity to expand his business aggressively. Although his rubber factory was razed by arson, his position as the world's leading rubber trader remained unassailable.

Lark Sye's family also diversified into other industries, including banking, insurance, plantation, and construction. But rubber procession and trade remained its core businesses. As the helmsman of the family business, most decisions were made by him alone. His business acumen, audacity, and luck all combined to make Aik Hoe such a spectacular success, despite the volatility of the rubber trade.

Of course, as a typical Chinese family entrepreneur, Tan Lark Sye's success was not without limitations. The business was run as a family owned enterprise, and the patriarch could veto any proposals. The idea of bringing in professional talents who were not related to the family was completely alien to entrepreneurs like Tan. Still, because of his pragmatism and perseverance, Tan's enterprise continued as a shining star in S.E. Asia for tens of years.

In the early 1960s, the rubber business entered into a bad spell. Added to this, Tan's relationship with the Singapore government became quite strained. But Tan was not depressed, and decisively changed tack. He saw great potentials in paper products and the cement industry. In 1961, he set up Lima Paper Products Co Ltd, and built paper factories in Tampoi (Johore), Wellesley (Penang), and Kajang (Selangor), and Jurong (Singapore.) In 1963, he set up TASEK Cement Co Ltd, a joint venture which operated a large-scale cement plant in Perak. These two companies were subsequently listed on the Singapore and Malaysian Stock Exchanges, and were highly rated by investors.

From Tan Kah Kee Spirit to Nantah (Nanyang University) Spirit

Amongst the many successful and famous Chinese immigrants in the first half of the 20th century, Tan Kah Kee was uniquely prominent, for both his ability to amass wealth and philanthropic largess (especially for education).[2] He was the undisputed Number One Philanthropist. His personal philosophy that the best use for money was to spend it on society, and his strong belief that the most important element for a strong nation was universal education for its populace. These two principles influence many future rich Chinese, who tried to emulate his example.

Tan Lark Sye was to a great extent inspired by Tan Kah Kee's altruism. He began to donate generously towards Chinese education, culminating in his movement to establish the Nanyang University, the first Chinese university outside China.

Tan Kah Kee and Tan Lark Sye were compatriots and were related in many ways. Tan Lark Sye received his only few years of formal education in a school founded by Tan Kah Kee in Jimei, Fujian Province. Tan Lark Sye received his business apprenticeship in Tan Kah Kee's businesses. Throughout Tan Lark Sye's life, he regarded Tan Kah Kee as kin, idol, and elder, and tried very hard to follow in his footsteps.

Tan Kah Kee devoted all his life to education, and established several primary and high schools, as well as other educational institutions in Singapore and China. In 1921, he founded the Xiamen University. His educational institutions were funded primarily from his own wealth, supplemented by contributions from his close friends and others. Unfortunately, in the 1930s, his business empire showed signs of distress, culminating in their liquidation by bank creditors in 1934. He now had to rely on donations from alumni and former employees to fulfil his commitment in funding for these educational institutions.

Fortunately, by then Tan Lark Sye was already well-established in his business. He would always follow his mentor's advice, and help him fulfil his wishes. In 1939, the Jimei School Alumni held a fund-raising campaign, and collected S$300,000; Tan Lark Sye alone gave S$150,000. In 1941, Tan Kah Kee received another S$20,000 from Tan Lark Sye for the setting up of Nanqiao Institute of Education. Prior to the Japanese occupation of Singapore, Tan Lark Sye followed Tan Kah Kee's instruction to donate

S$700,000 to restore Jimei School in China, and to rejuvenate Fujian's economy.

Like Tan Kah Kee, Tan Lark Sye contributed not only to Chinese-language education, he also donated generously to the English schools. Tan Kah Kee had donated to the Anglo-Chinese School (founded by the American Methodist Church) and the government-funded Raffles Institute. Tan Lark Sye would do likewise. In 1950, when he took office as the chairman of the Chamber of Commerce, he raised S$500,000 for the newly established Malayan University, including his personal donation of S$300,000.[3]

Tan Kah Kee had long harboured a vision to found a local Chinese university. In 1918, the principal of Anglo-Chinese School proposed the setting up of a Anglo-Chinese Institute, to which Tan Kah Kee readily pledged to donate S$100,000 as a seed fund. However, due to the British authority's obstruction, the plan never materialised. But Tan Kah Kee's passion never waned, and three years later, he successfully established the Xiamen University in China. From then on, Tan Kah Kee never mentioned the setting up of a university in Singapore. His initial dream of a Singapore university would eventually come true through the efforts of his successors, led by Tan Lark Sye.

In 1953, Tan Lark Sye finally proposed the setting up Nanyang University, and kick-started it with a personal donation of five million dollars, plus a donation from Hokkien Association of 500 acres of land. Thus began the avalanche of financial donations from all sectors of the Chinese community in Singapore and Malaya. The movement was unstoppable, and the University was finally established in 1956.[4]

In the process of founding Nanyang University, the Chinese community manifested the spirit of hard work, personal sacrifices for the greater good of the masses, and audacity. This attitude gradually gained the enviable epithet of Nantah (i.e. Nanyang University) Spirit. Many years later, the founding prime minister of Singapore, Lee Kuan Yew, said, "If we lose the Nantah Spirit, the society of Singapore will be in trouble!"[5]

Glory and Downfall: Historical Setback

The British Colonial Office commented on Tan Lark Sye in 1949: "Tan Lark Sye is a prudent capitalist who is more interested in business than in politics."

Admittedly Mr. Tan Lark Sye was never very active in politics, especially party politics. But he was highly concerned with political developments.

Tan became engaged in community work as soon as his business gained a sound and firm footing. Since 1937, he was successively elected as chairman of the Rubber Trade Association of Singapore and the Rubber Manufacturers and Traders Association of Singapore. In 1941, before the breakout of the Pacific War and the Fall of Singapore, he was also elected the vice chairman of the Chinese Chamber of Commerce, one of whose main concerns then was to organise relief for China, which was being bullied by the Japanese militarists. When Singapore fell, he fled to Indonesia.[6]

In 1949, Tan Kah Kee decided to relocate to China, and Tan Lark Sye was chosen to succeed him as chairman of the Hokkien Association. In the following year, he was elected as the 26th chairman (1950–1951) of the Chamber of Commerce. By now, he was the undisputed leader of the Singapore Chinese.

Towards the end of 1950, the colonial government revised the Immigration Act to impose stringent regulations on issue of re-entry permits into Malaya and stringent restriction on new immigrants. These new measures provoked an uproar among the Chinese. Under the leadership of Tan Lark Sye, the Chamber of Commerce called for a general meeting of local Chinese and organisations to sign a joint letter of protests. At the same time, a task force was set up to study the issues of voting rights for Chinese. A memorandum was then presented to the government to lobby for citizenship for local Chinese. The memorandum made it clear that Singaporean Chinese were ready to severe political ties with China, and would only be loyal to Singapore, and Singapore alone. This petition was in effect a public declaration of the entire Chamber to dissociate themselves from their previous political allegiance to China.[7]

The Chamber continued to spearhead the arduous task of fighting for citizenship for local Chinese. At the same time, the Chamber also actively organised voters to register, to fight for the abolition of the language barriers in the legislative assembly of Singapore. The Chamber offered moral support and financial assistance to the Democratic Party to participate in the Legislative Assembly election in 1955. Although the Democratic Party suffered a crushing defeat, the Chamber's efforts in other areas fared well. In 1956, the Legislative Assembly passed a resolution on use of English, Malay, Chinese, and Tamil (an Indian dialect) as the official languages. In the same year, Chief Minister David Marshall also kept his promise to obtain the consent of the British authorities to draw up the Singapore Citizenship Act (1957). The Act offered some compromises in the provisions for citizenship applications which rendered some 220,000 China-born Singaporean Chinese eligible for Singapore citizenship.

Tan Lark Sye, the Chairman of the Chinese Chamber of Commerce played a pivotal role in all these political activities. In 1957, he led a delegation of Singaporean rubber traders to London to attend the British–Malayan rubber traders' convention, where he argued fervently on behalf of Singaporean and Malayan traders, and earned due respect from his Western counterparts. In the same year, he helped to set up the incorporation of the Malayan Rubber Union as the representative body of the rubber traders (Chinese or British) of Malaya, which unanimously elected him as the inaugural chairman.

With the establishment of the Nanyang University, Tan Lark Sye's reputation sky rocketed. The University was something that all overseas Chinese could be proud of. On March 30, 1958, tens of thousands of people turned up to witness the grand opening ceremony of the University. Tan went on stage to congratulate the University, and wished that its "songs and music would resonate for generations." Tan's name had now reached the summit.

From the very beginning Nanyang University faced all sorts of discrimination. Despite all this, the University grew rapidly and steadily. But before long, it was confronted with an even greater obstacle. In order to evaluate the degrees offered by the University, two reports by specialists were submitted to the government. The S.L. Prescott Report, and later, the Dr. Gwee Ah Leng Report. The first report summarily dismissed the University's degrees on the ground of its administrative flaws. The second report was less brash, but largely concurred with the first report's positions that Nanyang University ought to model itself after the Malayan University, that English should be more liberally used as medium of instruction, and finally that the University should eventually transform itself into a public-funded university.

Even though the Nanyang University Act had been in effect since 1959, the University Board was not set up in accordance with the Act, because the Gwee Ah Leng Report recommended a major amendment of the Act and to set up a provisional Board to take over and reorganise the University. The negotiations between the government and the University over the issue of reorganisation were deadlocked over the issue of the board composition. However, the Board was eventually set up in July 1962 and was chaired by Tan Lark Sye. The government appointed its representatives to the Board, but would not agree to fund the University unless it carried out its revamp in accordance with the recommendations of the Gwee Ah Leng Report.

By 1963, the government representatives continued in their stance in adopting the review report as the blueprint for revamp, while the University was firm on its own agenda of continued reform which aimed to increase efficiency and raise the academic standards, while insisting on the original principle of "upholding the Chinese language as the main medium of instruction." The government wanted to have 12 representatives on the board, same number as the sponsors. But Tan Lark Sye insisted that the government could have only 3, as provided by the Act.

The same year, Singapore entered into a period of political turmoil. Tan, whose main concern was Nanyang University, and not politics, was unwittingly dragged into the political struggle. In 1963, Tan resigned from his chairmanship of Nanyang University Board. This was a watershed in his life.

Deeds and Merits Recorded in the Annals of History

We have kept track of Tan Lark Sye and his imprints over the passage of time. The impression we gained is one of an unusually successful entrepreneur, who was straight-forward, frank, audacious, and possessed a great sense of social responsibility and historical mission. He regarded himself as Tan Kah Kee's successor both as a philanthropist and as the protector of Chinese education. Put simply, Tan Lark Sye was, spiritually speaking, Tan Kah Kee's reincarnation.

Tan Kah Kee and Tan Lark Sye continued to exert influence after their death. Many tried to emulate them in promoting education. This is a good example of a historical truism that many events are constituents in a continuum. A certain cause may experience peaks and valleys, or even dark abyss, yet it doesn't die, but continues to play out the drama.

Tan Lark Sye has left us for 25 years. The shadows of him never leave us, they do not even fade away. The University established by him was incorporated into the National University of Singapore in 1980. The name may have vanished, but the grandeur of the edifices in Yunnan Garden is a constant reminder to us that there have been sweat and toil, anxiety, laughters and tears in this now seemingly extremely peaceful garden. Of the 21 batches of over 10,000 graduates, almost all of them have been serving the Singapore and Malaysia community with their tertiary training, while some of them went overseas to further their studies. All of them strive for achievements in their respective fields.

The contributions of Tan Lark Sye to education are indisputable. The setting up of a Chinese language department in both Singapore and Malayan Universities and the setting up of the Chinese University in Hong Kong could be indirectly attributed to the catalyst effect from Nanyang University. In consequence the Malaysian Chinese community attempted to set up an independent university. Though they did not succeed in this, they managed to establish the Southern College, and are now actively organising for the New Era College. All these efforts could be attributed to their passion to emulate Tan Lark Sye in his setting up of Nanyang University, and to emulate Lark Sye's predecessor Tan Kah Kee.

Tan Lark Sye succeeded in establishing Nanyang University, but he had to face many frustrations and setbacks, mainly because of unfavourable political ambience. To many, English seemed to be natural choice for education's instruction medium, and for working, technical, and legal language. But now, as China's power and influence ascend, many S.E. Asia governments are less xenophobic towards the Chinese language and culture. If Tan Lark Sye were still alive and active today, what fate will confront him?

Historians often take a very long time to come to consensus, most of the time they never do. Generations later, what will the storytellers say about Tan Lark Sye?

Endnotes

1. For further reading about the rise and fall of Tan Lark Sye's businesses, refer to *Familism and Enterprise: The Business World of Tan Lark Sye*, by Lim How Seng
2. *On Tan Kah Kee's Support of Education*, by Wang Zengbing and Yu Gang (Fujian Educational Press, 1981), and *Tah Kah Kee: the Making of An Overseas Chinese Legend* (Singapore, Oxford University Press, 1987)
3. *Special Commemorative Issue on the 80th Anniversary of the Singapore Chinese Chamber of Commerce and Industry*, page 347
4. *"25 Years of Nanyang University", A Compilation of Historical Literature of the Nanyang University*, by Yi Xing (Nanyang University Alumni Association in Malaya, 1990) pages 11–25
5. Kuala Lumpur, *Sin Chew Jit Poh*, 31 January 1993
6. *Brief Biography os Southeast Chinese Elites*, by Tan Ee Leong, Singapore 1977
7. *Shifts in the National Identification of the Chinese in Malaysia and Singapore, 1945–1959*, by Chui Kwei Chiang, Nanyang Society of Singapore, 1990

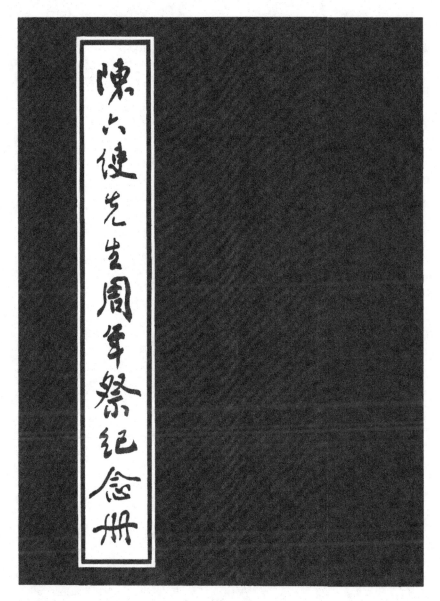

"Commemorative book on the 1st Anniversary of Mr. Tan Lark Sye's Death: A "book without words".

Chapter 5

The Corporate World
of Tan Lark Sye

Lim How Seng

Tan Lark Sye's Rubber Empire

His childhood and journey across the Southern Seas

Tan Lark Sye was born on June 7, 1897, in Jimei Town, Tong'An county, Fujian Province of China, two years after the war against Japanese aggression in 1894–1895 (Sino-Japanese War). In his childhood, he witnessed some great changes, such as the failed Constitution Reform and Modernisation, spearheaded by Kang Youwei and Liang Qichao, and the successful Sun Yat-sen-led Revolution of 1911, which overthrew the imperial Qing Dynasty and the founding of the Republic of China.

Tan was born into a poor family, and both his parents died on the same day when he was still young. His childhood was extremely miserable. He was sixth among seven brothers, hence his name Lark Sye (Lark meaning six or sixth in Hokkien dialect.) His five elder brothers are Wen Yi, Wen Qin, Wen Que, Ke Dou, and Wen Zhi, in that order. His younger brother was named Wen Zhang.

He grew up in a village and made a living on fishing and cutting firewood. Of the seven brothers, only the third and the youngest brothers attended primary school. Third brother (Wen Que) also dropped out of school after their parents' death. Thanks to Tan Kah Kee, who had set up the Jimei School in their hometown in 1913, Lark Sye and youngest brother Wen Zhang were able to continue their schooling free.

Third brother Wen Que was the first of the brothers to migrate, and moved to Malaya. Eldest brother Wen Yi allowed him to leave

China mainly because he was prone to seasickness and not suited for fishing. This was soon followed by fourth, fifth, and youngest brother. In 1916, Lark Sye also left China.

Without friends and relatives, the Tan brothers could only turn to Tan Kah Kee to find jobs at Tan Kah Kee's rubber plantation and factory. As principals of Jimei School, Tan Kah Kee and his younger brother Tan Kin Hian always took care of the welfare of students from the school and would employ many of them. Tan Lark Sye and youngest brother Wen Zhang therefore joined elder brother Wen Que to work in Tan Kah Kee's companies. The 4th brother, Ke Dou, worked for Tan Kah Kee for a while before leaving to partner a friend to set up freight and remittance business.

Tan Keong Choon, nephew of Tan Kah Kee, remembered how Tan Lark Sye recounted his story at a meeting of the Rubber Industry Association of Singapore in the early 1960s. Tan Lark Sye at first went to see Tan Kin Hian (vice principal of Jimei School), who sent him to work in a rubber plantation in Malaya. Half a year later, he was redeployed to work as a junior foreman at a rubber factory in Singapore. In those days he only wore wooden clogs and shorts at work, and his monthly wage was just four straits dollars, but accommodation and food were provided for. Lark Sye was very thrifty, and each month he would spend only one dollar: on cigarettes and haircut.[1]

There was a set of rules to be observed by workers in Tan Kah Kee rubber factories, such as obedience, and strictly no gambling, fighting, stealing, and sabotage etc.[2] Tan Lark Sye learned rubber processing, grading of sheets, and organising and managing of rubber factories. Third brother Wen Que managed a rubber plantation while operating a small provisions shop at the plantation. Work experience at the rubber factories and plantations, plus their keen observation of the rubber trade practice, proved an important advantage when the Tan brothers set up their own business.

The history of Aik Hoe rubber company

Tan Lark Sye started his own business in the mid 1920s. Around 1925, the rubber market was booming worldwide. Thanks to the implementation of Stevenson's plan to restrict rubber production in 1922, prices steadily increased, peaking at 200 straits dollars per hundredweight or 1.8 dollars per pound by end 1925. The lucrative rubber market lured dozens of Tan Kah Kee's employees to quit their jobs to start their own businesses, including Tan Lark Sye and his brother.

According to Tan Eng Joo, Lark Sye's nephew and former chairman of the Singapore Chamber of Commerce and Industry, the Tan brothers' business venture was helped by then Comprador of the BSBC Bank, See Teong Wah.[3] Their first business was named Lian Hoe Rubber Shop.

The Tan brothers' business did not get any help from Tan Kah Kee, though they knew each other well and were from the same town in China, quite unlike Lee Kong Chian. Lee hailed from a different, neighbouring county called Nan'An, but he attracted Tan Kah Kee's attention as he worked at a senior management level in Tan Kah Kee's business. Tan Kah Kee appreciated Lee Kong Chian so much that Lee became his son-in-law. On the other hand, Tan Lark Sye and brother were just two of Tan Kah Kee's many ordinary workers, who failed to attract special attention from their boss.

Initially the Tan brothers were somewhat apprehensive about starting their business, and adopted a defensive strategy. They did not quit their jobs, and instead employed a retired manager to run the business on their behalf. The manager was experienced but not very energetic, due to advanced age. The business thus suffered losses in the midst of a booming rubber market. The brothers decided that the youngest one, Wen Zhang, should resign from his job to run Lian Hoe. However, due of Wen Zhang's lack of experience, business did not improve. Finally, Lark Sye and Wen Que resigned from their jobs to focus on their business.

By 1928, the Tan brothers' rubber business was on a firm footing. Aik Hoe now owned an import/export business and two rubber factories: one at Paya Lebar (Kim Chuan Road Rubber Factory) and the other at Kampong Bahru. Their wholesale business, called Lian Hoe, was located at 39 Beach Road.[4]

The Great Depression of the 1930s caused catastrophic damages to major rubber dealers worldwide, and the businesses of overseas

Chinese rubber magnates, including Lim Nee Soon's and Tan Kah Kee's collapsed. Demand for rubber was reduced drastically, causing the price to fall to as low as 7 cents per pound in 1932, from its peak of $1.80 in 1925. Many rubber plantations stopped tapping, and factories shut down.

There are always people, albeit rare, who could turn adversities into opportunities. Tan Lark Sye and Lee Kong Chian were two outstanding examples. They survived due to their relatively small scale of investments. The demise of bigger players gave them opportunities and they both wisely chose the strategy of chasing large volumes while sacrificing margins. Their businesses grew, in the Great Depression!

In 1933, Tan Kah Kee scaled back on his businesses. His rubber factories in Singapore and Malaya were leased to his former employees. The rubber factory that was leased to Aik Hoe. Profits so gained by Tan Kah Kee were to be used for the funding of Xiamen University and Jimei School.

By 1938, Aik Hoe already became one of the largest rubber traders in Singapore and Malaya. It was also one of a handful of Chinese rubber traders who managed to break the foreigners' control of rubber trade, and it since then also set up representative offices in New York and London. It also purchased more rubber plantations.

In October 1938, Aik Hoe was reorganised into a private limited company, with a registered and paid-up capital of 1 million dollars.[5] The company was also relocated to 31 Circular Road. In 1937, Tan Lark Sye was elected chairman of the Rubber Trade Association of Singapore. In 1940, Aik Hoe's registered capital was increased to 2 million dollars, while the paid-up capital remained at 1 million dollars.

Since 1938, Aik Hoe took huge loans from the British Mercantile Bank to fund its expansion, reaching $1.5 million in 1940.[6]

During WW2, Tan Lark Sye sought refuge in Indonesia, and Aik Hoe's business was suspended.

After the war, Aik Hoe resumed its business on September 5, 1945. Around this time, his nephew Eng Joo, son of Ke Dou, returned from his studies in the U.S., to join Aik Hoe. He was widely speculated to be Tan Lark Sye's successor-designate.

Soon after the war, the British government imposed martial law in Singapore, and rubber became a controlled item. The British set up a Rubber Buying Unit that monopolised rubber trade. All Singapore and Malayan rubber suppliers had to sell their rubber to this Unit at a ridiculously low price of 36 cents per pound. The British government only lifted its monopoly on New Year's Day of 1947.

Aik Hoe moved to 6 Raffles Quay (also called Lau Pa Sat) in September 1946.

With the resumption of free trade, rubber prices picked up gradually. By 1949, rubber was traded at around 50 cents per pound. In February that year, Aik Hoe increased its paid-up capital to two million dollars,[7] and in September, moved to 5-7 Beach Road.

On June 25, 1950, the North Korean army marched into South Korea, and the Korean War broke out. The war backers went into a buying frenzy of rubber, which was a strategic material. This golden age of rubber trade saw its price rising from 95 cents (in June 1950) to $1.20 (July), $1.47 (August), and peaking at $2.18 in January 1951.

Just as all seemed exceptionally well, Aik Hoe's factory in Kim Chuan Road was set on fire by arsonists on July 27, 1950.

The factory at that time employed 1,200 workers, 800 males and 400 females. The fire started from the third floor of the main warehouse before quickly spreading out of control. Only the office building was spared. The entire factory was gutted along with approximately 5,000 tons of stock rubber. Total estimated losses amounted to $10 million.[8]

Aik Hoe was by then such a pivotal player that news of the fire caused the weakening rubber to immediately rebound.[9] Fortunately, the factory was insured for $7 million underwritten by the New Zealand Insurance Company, American Insurance Underwriters Ltd, Asia Insurance Company, and Wing On Fire and Marine Insurance Company.[10] The loss was trimmed to $3 million after being offset from insurance compensations. Soon after, the Tan brothers obtained a loan of $7 million from the Mercantile Bank to rebuild the factory.

While the fire caused a huge financial loss to Aik Hoe, it remained robust due to the exceptional profits from the Korean War.

In the 1950s, Tan Lark Sye was at his peak in terms of his business and his public life. In addition to rubber trade, the Tan brothers also dabbled in banking and insurance before the Korean War. Tan Lark Sye served as a director of Overseas Chinese Bank. His brother Wen Que served as board chairman of Asia Insurance Company Ltd and Asia Life Insurance Company Ltd. Apart from holding the chairmanship of the Rubber Association of Singapore since 1937, Lark Sye was also elected as chairman of the Singapore Chinese Chamber of Commerce and Industry in 1950. In 1953, he spearheaded efforts to establish the Nanyang University.

The 1960s saw the founding of Malaysia, with Singapore joining at a later date. Indonesia violently opposed this development with its Confrontation policy. Singapore's re-export trade suffered greatly as a result, with the rubber industry bearing the brunt of Indonesia's action, because rubber factories in Singapore had long been relying largely on importing raw rubber (wet rubber) from Indonesia. Aik Hoe's business suffered, and it started diversifying its investments.

Tan Lark Sye's Leadership Image, Business and Economic Thoughts

In 1949 Tan Lark Sye was a conservative in the eyes of the British colonial government. Here is a note of the Colonial Department on Tan Lark Sye: "In the absence of Tan Kah Kee, the Hokkien Huay Kuan (Hokkien Association) appointed Tan Lark Sye as its chairman and the leader of the (Hokkien) faction. Tan Lark Sye is a scrupulous capitalist who is more interested in business than in politics. His rise in fortune should be credited to his first job that Tan Kah Kee offered to him."[11]

This note also illustrates Tan Lark Sye's status within the Hokkien faction in the post-war years. When Tan Kah Kee decided to relocate in China in 1950, he made arrangement for his successor to be the leader of the Hokkien Association, which he had led for almost 20 years. The two short-listed candidates were his son-in-law Lee Kong Chian and Tan Lark Sye, both now prominent in the rubber trade and the Hokkien community. On the eve of his departure for China, Tan Kah Kee announced his decision that he had chosen Tan Lark Sye to be his successor, who was then swiftly elected as chairman of the Association in 1950.[12]

Tan Kah Kee had thought Lee Kong Chian was too law-abiding. In fact, Lee showed little interest in clan politics, though he had always supported his father-in-law Tah Kah Kee, especially during the tussle for chairmanship with See Teong Wah in 1929. Lee was also regarded as better-educated, with broader view of community welfare, not restricting himself to the Hokkien clan. In 1948, Lee had established a good relationship with the British High Commissioner for S.E. Asia, Malcolm Macdonald, and was engaging in serious discussions with Tan Cheng Lock (of Malaya) over the issue of political future of the Chinese in post-war Singapore and Malaya. In contrast, Tah Kah Kee was conscious that Tan Lark Sye had little education and could not speak English, and was therefore more suited to faction politics. Tan Kah Kee felt that Tan Lark Sye was more audacious and obstinate, and would pursue his mission doggedly, even to the extent of breaking the law. An example of his impulsive response was his remitting of 70 million China dollars to China, stating clearly that Jimei School could tap the fund, when needed.[13]

Tan Lark Sye very much resembled Tan Kah Kee in terms of personality, temperament, and interpersonal relationship. Tan Kah Kee would devote all his fortune for education, care for his hometown, and fellow countrymen, virtually with no limits. He was bold in making decisions and taking responsibilities. In short, Tan Kah Kee was almost a dictatorial clan elder, entrepreneur and community leader.

Obviously influenced by Tan Kah Kee, Tan Lark Sye spearheaded the establishment of Nanyang University. Both of them were confident, optimistic, risk-taking, not dodging responsibilities, and ready to lead by example: essence of a successful entrepreneur.

But there were also some discernible negative traits in him: he was stubborn, dictatorial, and emotional. For instance, he would unconditionally help someone of his fancy.[14]

Tan Lark Sye spent most of his life in the rubber business. Under the British rule, the Chinese businessmen were relegated to subordinate roles while the global rubber trade centres were based in London and New York. The British and American Rubber Association and the Western Rubber Traders Association in Singapore set the rules of play favourable to themselves. Both Tan Lark Sye and Lee Kong Chian therefore led the fight for trade autonomy and against protectionism. Lark Sye and Kong Chian spent almost their whole lives to relocate the international rubber trade centres from consumer countries to producer countries like Singapore and Malaya.

After the war, the British and American rubber traders often complained to the colonial government about inferior quality of the rubber shipped and demanded compensations. The government was pressured to introduce the Rubber Packing and Shipping Control Act under which the Malayan Rubber Export Registration Bureau was set up, which was empowered to impose heavy fines. Since this act was implemented, the number of cases of claim increased rapidly. In 1956 alone, the Bureau received 204 cases, making life very difficult for local traders.[15]

As chairman of the Rubber Association, Tan Lark Sye led a delegation of five members representing the rubber traders of Singapore (other members being Tan Eng Joo, Ng Quee Lam, Soon Kwee Choon, and Tan Puay Chui) to attend a joint conference of British and Malayan rubber traders in London. Before leaving Singapore, Tan Lark Sye said the delegation wanted to "see how and how much they are going to suck our blood".[16]

He said, "We have all come down with tuberculosis. We are all doomed if we cannot find a new cure. The purpose of this trip is to find the cure.

"The western businessmen in Singapore and Malaya have long usurped the position of market leaders in the rubber industry from their Chinese counterparts, by fair or foul means. In 1953, before I was elected chairman of the Rubber Traders Association, the western businessmen instigated the government to hastily set up the Rubber Export Registration Bureau, to gain unfair control of the rubber industry. Take for example, the case of any shipment deemed to be different from what was specified, the shippers' licence will be revoked in addition to a heavy fine of $25,000 plus two years' imprisonment. These rules are obviously drawn up to disadvantage the locals.

"The Bureau's expenses amounted to hundreds of thousands of dollars a year, paid by the local people. But, instead of serving the local people, it colluded with foreigners to hurt the local people. Do we need such a traitorous government organ?"

"In theory, the Bureau was set up to facilitate rubber trade between Singapore and Malaya and the rest of the world. But, after it was set up, orders had been shrinking, and traders had to slash prices, by as much as 2–3 pence per pound. The local traders had little recourse, because the Bureau always favoured them. How can we survive?"

"As I said before, we have all come down with tuberculosis. We still face pressure to slash prices. The die is cast. We have to stake all that we have for this Battle Royal."

"I have the honour to have been the chairman of the two rubber associations in Singapore for over 20 years, the combined assets of the two associations now amount to millions of dollar, which are our only support. I truly fear that when we die, all these assets will also disappear. So the aim of this trip is to find out how and how much they plot to suck our blood. I am not at all confident that my personal dream of demolishing the Bureau will come true."[17]

Tan Lark Sye took the opportunity of attending the London meeting to visit Europe, U.S.A., Japan and Hong Kong. This was his first tour of these major cities, and it helped to broaden his outlook. At a welcome dinner at the Tanjong Rhu Club upon his return, he spoke about his gainful experience.

He reported that the greatest progress made in the conference was to make their British counterparts realise the important position of the Rubber Association of Singapore, and that views of Chinese traders in Singapore deserve greater respects from the British. The

British manufacturers admitted the British rubber retailers in London had taken unfair advantage of the existing situation. The Singapore team also suggested that the British manufacturers set up a branch office in Singapore, to facilitate ex-warehouse trade.[18]

Soon the Rubber Association and the Western Rubber Traders Association got together to establish a general rubber association. Tan Lark Sye forwarded a proposal which included rubber traders of all races in the general association in order to enhance its international status.[19] The delegation thus achieved a major breakthrough by wrestling the initiative in rubber dealing for the Singapore–Malayan rubber industry. The Chinese traders started to gain the respect of local-based western traders and European and American traders.

On this trip, Tan Lark Sye also saw how the Malaya Rubber Export Registration Bureau and the British trade attache to Singapore and Malaya sided with the British exporters' agents. He asked, "Why do we have to spend money to support people who look after other people's interests? Can they not be replaced?"[20]

Tan also mentioned that "some representatives sent to the rubber conference in Indonesia were academics with high degrees, whose research proved that rubber prices should not exceed 60 cents per pound." He concluded that Singapore and Malayan rubber industry should not rely on these foreigners. "To survive, we need our own academics."[21]

During his trip, Tan noticed that the United States and Europe had made spectacular progress after the war, but such progress did not seem to benefit the third world. He also lamented that Singapore and Malayan corporations lagged far behind their western counterparts.

"Our trip was like a bunch of countrymen going to town," said Tan. "The infrastructure and development of industry and commerce in Singapore lag far behind the West. They could employ 200–300 thousand workers in just one mechanised factory, producing tens of billions of dollars turnover, and tens of millions dollars profits. This is more than what the entire Singapore can produce. Are Singapore capitalists entitled to call themselves such? Five percent profit margin for a big Western company could easily amount to millions of dollars. Yet they complain that margins are too low. We cannot find one single such capitalist in Singapore. But our workers and even the government have postured to overthrow the capitalists. In my view, if the West continued to develop this way and suck us dry, the capitalists here would soon die of natural deaths, without government intervention."[22]

He mentioned that after WW2, neo-colonialism led governments to implement food rationing, foreign exchange control, and economic aid for less developed countries. While these measures seemed benign, they actually harmed the people by restricting their production, causing perennial poverty.[23]

In 1958, the Import and Export Company of China claimed that rubber from Singapore and Malaya was inconsistent in quality. As chairman of the Rubber Association, Tan Lark Sye advised its members to improve their relationship with their Chinese partners, as China had by now become the second largest buyer of rubber from Singapore and Malaya. He wrote to the Import and Export Company to explain that the rubber being complained about had come from Indonesia, Borneo and Thailand. He suggested a meeting with them.[24]

In comparison with his tough remarks before leaving for the London conference the previous year, the letter to the Chinese company was written with diplomatic finesse, with a hint of apologies between lines. This demonstrates Tan's two different approaches as a leader of the rubber industry. To the British and American rubber traders, he carried with him the burden of Chinese businessmen's long suffering under the colonists' exploitation. His mission was to fight for justice. The relationship was purely non-personal, and based on contracts and law. In contrast, he took a mild and friendly stand when he dealt with the complaints from China, possibly because he still harboured a strong passion for his motherland. Such sentiments made him adopt a clan-like attitude towards the China counterparts. Disputes between kinsmen should be addressed in a harmonious atmosphere, and not through legal battles. In his letter to the China company, he said "We can always meet in person to sort out all problems," implying that no problems between kins-men could not be settled.

The Structure and Management of Tan Lark Sye's Family Enterprise

Aik Hoe Group adopted the typical Chinese family way of business management, whereby ownership and management are integrated. We shall analyse the management of the Tans' family enterprise from its capital structure, form of investments, management struc-ture and ways of conducting business.

Capital structure of Aik Hoe

In the beginning, the Tans' family business was run by the brothers. After the war, their children joined as managers, eventually covering the enterprise with family members at all levels. The Tan family numbered over 200 in Singapore and Malaya.

Among the five brothers who migrated to Singapore, the most well-known were third brother Wen Que, fourth brother Ke Dou, sixth brother Lark Sye, and the youngest Wen Zhang. Little-known fifth brother Wen Zhi apparently became a small shareholder of Aik Hoe in 1938, and the shareholders' register indicated that he was living with third brother Wen Que. Second brother Wen Qin did not come to Singapore, but his sons Eng Ho and Eng Chin came over. Eldest brother Wen Yi stayed behind to watch over their ancestral home.

Aik Hoe Company Limited was the flagship company, and dealt mainly with rubber processing, packing, distribution imports and exports.

Aik Hoe was established in 1925, as a private limited company with a registered and paid-up capital of $1 million. On the eve of WW2, its registered capital was increased to $2 million. The paid-up capital remained unchanged until 1949, when it was topped up to $2 million, with no changes thereafter.

Aik Hoe's capital resources were much larger than any other major rubber traders in Singapore at the time of the Korean War. In comparison, the registered and paid-up capital of Ko Teck Kin's Chia Hsing was $800,000 and $400,000 respectively, and for Lau Tai San's Ta Yu, they were $1 million and $500,000 respectively. The majority of Aik Hoe's shares were held by members of the extended Tan family.

The allocated number of shares of each of the Tan families was fixed since the company was registered in 1938, and saw little change since then. The initial allocation of shares to the founders had been largely observed with no squabbles. The transfer of shares took place only within each of the family off-shoots, with no records of such transfers beyond the family off-shoots.

Forms of clan capital investment

Aik Hoe Group is primarily engaged in rubber processing and import-export trading. Apart from its own large-scale factory in Kim Chuan Road dealing with processing and trading, the Tan brothers also set up the following subsidiary companies and joint ventures that dealt with rubber and commodities trading:

(a) Lian Hoe Company Limited was a rubber wholesaler established in the same year as Aik Hoe. The founder of the company was the seventh brother Wen Zhang who also became Lian Hoe's General Manager. After the War, the company operated from the same premises as Aik Hoe's, which is 5-7 Beach Road.

(b) Hiap Hoe Company Limited was engaged in rubber processing and import–export trade. It was founded by the Simei Company, which was owned by the Wong Quee Lam family, in 1947 with a registered capital of $945,000. The Tan family started acquiring shares of the company in 1954, and its registered and paid-up capital were eventually increased to $4 million and $3 million, respectively. At the end of 1956, the Tan family formally acquired the company and handed the running of Hiap Hoe to the second generation members of the second, third, and sixth brothers. However, Aik Hoe remained the largest shareholder by holding 600 shares (at $1,000 per share).

(c) Ee Cheong Company Limited was a joint venture established in 1950, with Aik Hoe as majority shareholder. The directors of the company included Chang Ming Thien (former president of Hui Bai Mei Group), Tan Eng Jin (son of the second Tan brother), Tan Eng Ghee and Tan Eng Wah (sons of sixth Tan brother). The company dealt with shipping commodities like rubber, grains and grocery, mining and remittance. Its headquarters was sited at 65 Middle Road, with branches in Penang, Jakarta, Medan, Banjarmasin and Hong Kong.

(d) Chip Hoe Company Limited was established in 1956 with registered and paid-up capital of $100,000 each. As of 1962, its registered and paid-up capital were increased to $2 million and $1,644,000. It was owned by Tan Lark Sye's second son Eng Ghee. In 1962, Tan Lark Sye's first son Eng Wah joined the company as a minority shareholder. The company's registered address was the same as Aik Hoe Company.

(e) Hua Aik Company Limited was established in the same year as Chip Hoe Company Limited, with the two sons of Lark Sye, Eng Ghee and Eng Wah, as directors. The company's address was also the same as Aik Hoe Company.

The Tan family also owned quite a few rubber plantations in Malaya, including a rubber plantation of more than 3,000 acres at Gelang Patah, in Johore, Malaya. The Tan family was also involved with building, insurance, banking, and paper making.

In 1946, Tan Eng Joo, the only son of the fourth brother, graduated from the Massachusetts Institute of Technology with a Master of Science degree in Structural Engineering. He served as managing director at Aik Hoe Company. The Tan family also set up Tan Eng Joo Engineering Company Limited, headed by Eng Joo himself, with Tan Boon Kak as Chairman, and Lark Sye, Eng Jin and Eng Hoe as directors. The company was contracted to build the tallest building in Singapore then, Asia Insurance Building. However, this project was plagued with difficulties in the piling works. As a result the company suffered a significant loss. Meanwhile, the Tan family established another construction company, Associated Builders, which was also presided over by Eng Joo.

Before the War, the Tan family already had some shares in the Asia Insurance Company Limited and Overseas Chinese Bank Ltd. By 1966, the Tan family held 16% of Asia Insurance Company Limited. Soon after the War, Tan Boon Kak became Chairman of both Asia Insurance and Asia Life Insurance Companies. When he passed away in 1966, Lark Sye took over; and after Lark Sye passed away, Tan Eng Jin succeeded him.

Tan Lark Sye also served as a director of the Overseas Chinese Bank from 1943 to 1972, as well as Chairman of Chiyu Banking Corporation Limited in Hong Kong. Tan Boon Kak was appointed as a director of the United Overseas Bank Ltd, and Eng Joo was appointed as a director of both Overseas Union Bank Ltd and Chung Khiaw Bank Ltd.

Since the 1960s, the Tan family diversified into different businesses, and geographically into Malaysia, through share purchases on the Stock Exchanges. The family owned over a million shares of Tasek Cement Company Limited in Perak, Malaysia, and Tan Lark Sye became its chairman.

Enterprise organisation and management methodology

Aik Hoe had a small, simple, and highly centralised organisation structure, depicted as below:

Shareholders (Family Members)
Board of Directors (Family Members)
Management (Family members as senior managers)

The Board of Directors usually comprised four to eight persons appointed among the family shareholders, while the senior management was appointed from the directors. This was a typical family business model, where ownership and management were integrated under one entity.

The Tan family also had representatives on the board of public companies in which the family held substantial shares. There were nine family members who were on the board of at least two public companies. They were family elders Tan Boon Kak and Tan Lark

Sye, the second brother's sons Eng Hoe and Eng Jin, the fourth brother's son Eng Joo, and Lark Sye's sons Eng Ghee, Eng Han, Eng Wah, and Eng Hsin.[25]

Directors of the Tan family enterprise were not appointed proportionally according to amount of share ownership. Taking the board of Aik Hoe for example, we could clearly see how the clan system played an important role within the family enterprise, leveraging the interests of the component families, and minimising conflicts of interest.

Among the directors, founders Tan Boon Kak and Lark Sye were listed by virtue of their seniority and the amount of shareholding. Three other directors, second brother's sons Eng Hoe and Eng Jin, and fourth brother's son Eng Joo, were minority shareholders with less than 500 shares apiece. This was probably the work of Lark Sye and his brothers to ensure a fair representation of the brothers and their children on the board. At first, only family members of the second, third, and sixth founding brothers were represented on the board. Later, when Eng Joo returned to Singapore from the States, he was appointed as a director, thereby allowing the fourth brother's family to be represented. Such a equitable representation allowed conflicts to be minimised, while also keeping talents within the family enterprise.

When a non-family director of Aik Hoe embezzled company funds in 1957, the board of directors was reorganised with the number of directors increased from five to seven, with Tan Lark Sye's second and seventh sons Eng Ghee and Eng Han being appointed as directors, resulting Lark Sye's family having three members on the board, the greatest number among the families. After Tan Boon Kak died in 1966, Lark Sye's eldest son Eng Wah took over the seat. When Lark Sye died in 1972, his fifth son Eng Soon became a director, and the fourth brother's son Eng Joo resigned as the managing director, and Lark Sye's eldest son Eng Wah became the chief.[26] Changes in board composition did not change the company share ownership. The Tan families therefore remained united as a family clan.

While they were still alive, Boon Kak and Lark Sye formed a highly harmonious and united team of top management. There existed a tacit understanding between them: Generally Boon Kak took charge of the rubber plantations, processing factories, and insurance business, while Lark Sye had a free hand in rubber trade. Lark Sye also readily accepted Boon Kak as the undisputed patriarch of the family and was always respectful of him. In 1939, when Lark Sye was campaigning for the construction of the building of the Chinese Chamber of Commerce and Industry, he offered to donate up to $50,000 in the name of his elder brother Boon Kak.[27]

On the social front, Tan Lark Sye played a more important role than his brother Boon Kak. Boon Kak held important positions in the second tier organisations within the Hokkien Clan, serving as chairman of both Tung Ann Association and the Tan ancestral shrine in the Bao Chi Temple. On the other hand, Lark Sye held high-ranking positions within the Hokkien Clan as well as the general Chinese community. At different times, he served as Chairman of the Hokkien Association, the Chinese Chamber of Commerce and Industry, Rubber Association of Singapore, and Rubber Trade Association of Singapore.

Among the second generation Tans, fourth brother's only son, Eng Joo, was hand-picked by Boon Kak and Lark Sye to be groomed as their successor. Born in 1919, Eng Joo received Chinese education during his childhood before entering the Anglo-Chinese School. In 1939 he graduated from the Massachusetts Institute of Technology with a bachelor degree in engineering. He was awarded a scholarship to further his studies in structural engineering, and graduated with a master's degree in 1943. During WW2, he worked as a researcher at the National Defence Research Committee at Princeton University. After the war he returned to Singapore and was appointed by Tan Lark Sye as the managing director of Aik Hoe. Later Eng Joo was elected chairman of the Rubber Association of Singapore as well as vice-chairman and chairman of the Chinese Chamber of Commerce and Industry for many years.

In Aik Hoe, Lark Sye was the supreme decision maker. Due to the volatile nature of the rubber market, he usually got very personally involved in rubber trading. According to Tan Ee Leong, former secretary of the Chinese Chamber of Commerce and Industry, Tan

Lark Sye's office table was laid with several telephone sets. He would answer all phone calls himself, without the service of a receptionist.[28]

Modus operandi

The success of Aik Hoe was largely attributed to having the trust and support of the Mercantile Bank ever since the early days of the enterprise. The Bank provided most of loans required for business. After the war, the bank again granted $4 million to Aik Hoe to resume its business. In 1950, when Aik Hoe's factory was set on fire, the bank provided Aik Hoe $7 million in October to rebuild the factory. With backing from the Mercantile Bank, Aik Hoe grew to become one of the top rubber traders in the world, on par with Lee Kong Chian's Nam Aik (Lee Rubber Company.) Later, local Chinese banks also provided credit facilities to Aik Hoe.

Unlike Nam Aik, Aik Hoe did not set up representative offices and rubber processing factories in the rubber producing countries. Instead, Aik Hoe operated through its partner Ee Cheong's branches in Penang, Jakarta, Medan, and Banjarmasin for the supply of rubber and other commodities. In addition, Aik Hoe also bought rubber from various wholesalers and retail sellers, and small plantation owners. The raw (or "wet") rubber from Malaya and Indonesia was shipped to Singapore for processing, packing and redistribution by Aik Hoe Factory to major European and American countries. Rubber from Thailand was exported directly by its rubber dealers in Bangkok. Aik Hoe had set up agencies in London and New York before the war to handle shipments direct to the U.K., and the U.S.A.

Conclusions

Summing up Tan Lark Sye's life, he built his world-leading rubber empire from scratch, in the presence of powerful and prominent players like Tan Kah Kee and Lee Kong Chian. Although he had only primary school education, he recognised the importance of education, and shouldered the mission of founding the Nanyang University. The thousands of Nanyang University graduates would prove to be the only Chinese-educated elites in S.E. Asia for many decades after Nanyang University became history in 1980.

During the colonial period, he fought alongside Lee Kong Chian against the foreign rubber dealers, and paved the way for the post-independence governments of Singapore and Malaya to fight for the relocation of the international rubber trade centres from the consuming countries to the producer countries.

Though his style of management was conservative, his business strategies were often innovative and pioneering. In a bid to break up the stranglehold of the British Empire's network of trade protectionism, Aik Hoe challenged the foreign exchange control policy imposed by the British colonial government in the 1950s.

Tan Lark Sye was an exceptional entrepreneur. His sacrifices for, and contributions to the community, especially in the areas of Chinese political rights and Chinese education, will be remembered for a very long time by very many in S.E. Asia, especially in Singapore and Malaysia.

Endnotes

1. *Oral History Interview with Mr. Tan Keong Choon,* by the author, Oral History Museum of Singapore, 1981
2. Author's *Singapore Chinese Community and Entrepreneurs*
3. *Oral History Interview with Mr. Tan Eng Joo,* by the author
4. *Industrial Survey of Singapore,* compiled by Tong Zida, Nanyang Industrial and Commercial Preparatory School, Singapore, 1982, Chapters 14–17 and 24–25
5. *Aik Hoe & Co Pte (AH),* Registry of of Companies Records (ROCR), 41/38
6. *Ibid*
7. *Ibid*
8. *Sin Chew Daily and Nan Yang Siang Pau,* 18 July 1950
9. *Nan Yang Siang Pau,* 18 July 1950
10. *Ibid*
11. *Colonial Office 917/184,* 22 June 1949, page 54
12. *Oral History Interview with Lim Soo Gan,* 1982, Volume 26
13. *Memoirs of An Overseas Chinese in Southeast Asia,* by Tan Kah Kee, Prairie Press, Hong Kong, reprinted in 1971, pages 345–346

14. *Tan Ee Leong,* page 164
15. *Annual Report of the Malayan Rubber Export Registration Board,* February 1956
16. *Hong Kong Daily News,* 12 May 1957
17. *Ibid*
18. *Ibid,* 25 June 1957
19. *Nanyang Siang Pau,* 16 August 1957
20. *Ibid,* 25 June 1957
21. *Ibid*
22. *Ibid*
23. *Ibid*
24. *Sin Chew Daily,* 22 May 1958
25. ROCR 41/38
26. *List of Members and Trades of Singapore Chinese Chamber of Commerce and Industry,* 1972, page 122
27. *Diamond Jubilee Celebration of the 60th Anniversary of Singapore Chinese Chamber of Commerce and Industry Commemorative Album,* 1966, page 279
28. *Tan Ee Leong,* page 157

Chapter 6

The Extraordinary Life of Tan Lark Sye

Au Yue Pak

Nothing withstands the ravages of time. The idyllic Nanyang University campus, shaded ubiquitously by *acacia confusa*, (known romantically as the "pining tree"), is now the Nanyang Technological University. Nanyang University's founder, Tan Lark Sye, has also long passed away; but his selfless sacrifices he made in founding the University will always be remembered, especially by Nanyang University's graduates.

Tan Lark Sye's founding of the University is particularly praiseworthy because like many migrants of that time he himself had only a few years of education.

Born into a Poor Family in Jimei Town, Tong'An County, Fujian

Tan Lark Sye, a distant nephew of the famous Tan Kah Kee was born on June 7, 1897 in Jimei. China was in a state of anarchy. The time was ripe for a revolution. Tan Lark Sye was the sixth of seven brothers. Of the seven brothers, only third brother Wen Que, Lark Sye, and youngest brother Wen Zhang were fortunate enough to receive a few years of basic education, financially supported by the other brothers who eked out a living by fishing and woodcutting. Extreme poverty forced four of the brothers to migrate to Singapore, mainly because Tan Kah Kee was there.

Working at Tan Kah Kee's Rubber Factory

Boon Kak (Wen Que) and Ke Dou came first; and both worked for Tan Kah Kee's plantations. Tan Lark Sye joined them later, and worked in Tan Kah Kee's rubber factory. Tan Lark Sye was 19 then. Although he was related to Tan Kah Kee, the former got no special treatment from the latter. Lark Sye started from the lowest level, doing menial tasks. But soon Tah Kah Kee noticed the diligence and sharp observational skills of this young man, and hence transferred him to work in the office.

Lark Sye had an open and generous disposition. With a natural flair for socialising, he befriended many influential people in the rubber industry. Although he was treated well by Tan Kah Kee, Lark Sye was determined to be his own master.

Establishing Aik Hoe Rubber Company

After having acquired enough experience, the Tan brothers decided to venture into their own business. To minimise the risks, they let their youngest brother Boon Cheong run the business, Lian Hoe Rubber Company, while the others continued to work for Tan Kah Kee. However their inexperience led to losses of profits. Tan Lark Sye then decided to leave his job at Khiam Aik Rubber Company to focus on running Lian Hoe. As a result, their business improved by leaps and bounds . In 1925, when Lark Sye was 29, the brothers set up another company, called Aik Hoe Rubber Company. The two companies shared a building along Beach Road. The brothers worked hard and intelligently, and the business grew steadily. Soon they set up a rubber factory in Kim Chuan Road, and acquired some plantations. That was how Aik Hoe evolved to become a comprehensive player of the rubber trade.

In 1938 Aik Hoe became a limited company and expanded rapidly. Tan Lark Sye, now recognised as an industry leader, opened branches in Malaya, Indonesia, and Thailand. The cautious and farsighted Lark Sye also diversified into banking, becoming a substantial shareholder of OCBC and UOB before WW2.

He was deeply influenced by Tan Kah Kee and emulated him. He held the traditional Chinese belief that one of the most valuable ways to serve the community was to contribute to education, especially for the poor.

Donation for Education and the War of Resistance against Japan

To requite the society, Tan Lark Sye made large donations to local schools. He later partnered Lee Kong Chian to set up the Chiyu Banking Corporation Limited in Hong Kong, whose profits would be remitted to Fujian Province, China, to fund Jimei School and Xiamen University.

The Marco Polo (Lugou) Bridge incident of July 7, 1937 aroused unprecedented patriotism in S.E. Asian Chinese. In 1938, the Nanyang China Relief Fund Union was set up in Singapore to raise funds for war relief in China, and Tan Kah Kee was elected as its chairman.

Tan Lark Sye actively participated in the campaign, and was elected as the Singapore representative. He donated generously to the fund.

In February 1942, Singapore fell to the Japanese militarists. Aik Hoe, like many businesses, was shut down. Tan Lark Sye sought asylum in Indonesia for about half a year, before returning to Singapore.

After the War ended in 1945, Tan Lark Sye resumed his business activity, and before long, his production was back to pre-war levels. In the following year, Lark Sye's U.S.A.-trained nephew Tan Eng Joo returned to Singapore, and was immediately appointed managing director of Aik Hoe.

Rubber Business Peaking in the 1950s

When the Korean War broke out, rubber prices sky–rocketed. Tan Lark Sye made tremendous profits from rubber trade, and soon became one of the two leading rubber traders, the other being Lee

Kong Chian. Tan then diversified into insurance and banking, by setting up Asia Insurance Company and, jointly with Lien Ying Chow, the Overseas Union Bank. Because Lark Sye was already a director of OCBC, and Boon Kak a director of UOB, the Tan family let Tan Eng Joo represent them at the OUB (Overseas Union Bank.)

In the early 1950s, Tan was one of the richest men in S.E. Asia. He donated generously to charities, especially education, and helped many new immigrants to set up successful businesses. He was inexhaustible. In the 1960s he helped to set up the Tasek Cement Factory in Ipoh and became its chairman.

When Tan Kak Kee left Singapore for China in 1949, Tan Lark Sye took over as the leader of the Chinese community in Singapore, and the Hokkien Association. Recognising the importance of education, he set up an educational foundation. The foundation helped to pay for the expansion of three schools, namely, Tao Nan, Ai Tong, and Chongfu, and the construction of Kong Hwa School and Nan Chiau Girls' High School. It also funded the construction of the Hokkien Huay Kuan building. In only a few years, the student population at the five schools swelled to 15,000.

During his presidency of the Chinese Chamber of Commerce, he often donated generously to education. He donated $300,000 to the University of Malaya, which was of the same amount as the Chamber did. Reliable sources told us that he was always ready to help schools in financial difficulties, including Malay and Tamil schools.

The Chinese Education Conundrum

Before the 1950s, the Chinese community of S.E. Asia had very close ties with China, especially regarding education. In those days high school graduates from the English stream could further their studies in the U.K., while those from Chinese stream could only go to China. Teachers in the English stream hailed largely from India and the UK, while most teachers in the Chinese stream came from China.

In October 1949, the People's Republic of China (PRC) was established. This caused all educational ties between Singapore and China to be completely cut off. Students could no longer go to China for further studies, and teachers from China could no longer be recruited.

This sea change in China revived an old dream of setting up a Chinese language university in Singapore, and one with such a dream was Tan Lark Sye. As early as 1918, before the establishment of Raffles College and the University of Malaya, Tan Kah Kee already thought of setting up a university in Singapore. In that year, Mr. Naya, the principal of an American missionary school, visited Tan Kah Kee in Singapore. They discussed education, and agreed that a local university should be set up, which would include courses in Chinese. Naya was tasked to draw up plans for the university, while Tan Kah Kee would raise funds required. Soon, Tan raised $500,000 for the project.

While they were still getting government approval for the project, they bought dozens of acres of suburban land for the campus. The government was phlegmatic, and eventually rejected the proposal on the pretext that it had its own plan to set up a university.

Advocating the Establishment of Nanyang University

In 1953, as the self-anointed successor of Tan Kah Kee, Tan Lark Sye began to plan seriously the setting up of a Chinese university in Singapore. His reasons are two-fold. First, he was concerned that the shrinking pool of the Chinese-educated talents was not being replenished by sources from China, especially school teachers. Secondly, the Chinese-educated high school leavers had nowhere to go for further studies, because those who opted to go to China would not likely to be permitted to return to Singapore.

On January 16, 1953, at a meeting of the Hokkien Association, Tan Lark Sye proposed the setting up of a Chinese university, and pledged to donate $5 million. The proposal was adopted, and very soon the entire Chinese community in Singapore, Malaya, and beyond was mesmerised.

As expected, the colonial government and certain pro-British quarters opposed the plan to set up a Chinese university. The first to make his stand was Sir Sydney Caine, the Vice Chancellor of University of Malaya (in Singapore, first established in October 1949). He argued that it was not necessary to set up Nanyang University because his university would be setting up a Chinese faculty. He caveated that graduates from Chinese high schools would need to improve their English to be admitted to the University of Malaya.

Caine's view was questioned by a Chinese community heavy-weight (in Malaya), Sir Tan Cheng Lock, then chairman of the Malaya Chinese Association. Sir Tan argued that the proposed university would not compete with the University of Malaya, but rather complement it to meet the increasing enrolment of school leavers in Singapore and Malaya.

The bigger obstacle was the government's stand that Singapore needed only one university. But the dogged Tan Lark Sye was relent-less in his campaign. After several meetings with Sir William Goode, then Governor of Singapore, the government realised that the movement was unstoppable, partly due to the significant change of the Chinese community's insistence on their civil and political rights. So, the government reluctantly accepted Tan's plan.

At the final meeting with Tan, Governor Goode said, "The inten-tion to set up an institution of higher learning is good. But you'll need a huge sum of money. Regretfully, the government is unable to support you in this." Tan responded, "Education should be made available to all. Our university will be open to students from all races. As for the funds, we do not need the government's financing; we will raise the fund all by ourselves." Soon after this meeting, Nanyang University was finally incorporated on May 5, 1953, as "Nanyang University Limited."

Donations from all over S.E Asia

When the news broke out all the Chinese people in S.E. Asia were jubilant. People from all social strata began to donate money, or help in other ways enthusiastically. The contribution to the cause by the Malays and Indians were particularly moving. Equally touching deeds were fund raising rides by the trishaw drivers. All clans and associations joined in. The Hokkien Association made a spectacular donation of 550 acres of land to be used as the campus, in addition to $600,000 to build the Grand Auditorium.

Lin Yutang Affair

In the course of the establishment of Nantah (Nanyang University), the most distressing blow to Tan Lark Sye was the Lin Yutang Affair.

In 1954 the University invited Lin Yutang to be the inaugural President to oversee its establishment and administration. Lin Yutang brought in a team of scholars he had personally recruited to Nantah. Lin, who had been living in the West for many years, was hardly familiar with Singapore's latest political development. Before leaving for Singapore, Lin made a public statement to foreign correspondents that his goal was to build Nantah into an anticommunist bastion outside China. This added further complications to the already politicised controversies about the setting up of the University. Tan Lark Sye and his supporters were strictly apolitical. Their mission was simple and pure: education.

After his arrival in Singapore, Lin boasted about his desire to position Nantah as a top class university, and proceeded to ask for $20 million to start running the university. Tan Lark Sye, then Chairman of the Board of Directors, was appalled by such a request. Tan's position was that the initial wish of the Chinese community was to establish just an ordinary university, at least in the early stage.

The two opposing views were so divergent that any reconciliation was obviously impossible. Tan eventually paid $300,000 from his own pocket as severance pay for Lin and his team.

The departure of Lin Yutang did not impede the scheduled opening of the University. It recruited a new team of scholars for the university faculties. Pre-university classes were opened in June 1955, paving the way for the official opening of the University on the following year.

The Opening of Nanyang University

After three years of labour, everything was ready in the Yunnan Garden campus for the official opening. In early 1956, the first university classes commenced.

Tan Lark Sye chaired the University's Executive Committee from its commencement till his retirement in 1963. He spared no efforts in caring for the University. Whenever the university was unable to pay the staff salaries on time, Tan would advance his own money to the university as emergency funding.

When Nanyang University was merged with the National University of Singapore in 1980, it had nurtured nearly 20,000 graduates for Singapore, Malaysia, and other parts of S.E. Asia. One must not forget that it wasn't just money, Tan Lark Sye had also put in countless hours of hard work, and gone through insufferable mental effort, for the cause of universal education.

Fight for Citizenship and Language Rights

In the 1950s, during his presidency and special directorship at the Chamber of Commerce, Tan Lark Sye was committed to opposing the language restrictions at the proceedings of the legislative assembly which allowed only English to be used. English was then the sole language at all levels of government. Only candidates who were well versed in English had the opportunity to be elected into the legislature or the City Council.

Most Singaporeans were unhappy with the inferior status of the local languages other than English. In 1955, Tan Lark Sye and all the directors of the Chinese Chamber of Commerce forcefully voiced their protest over the language restriction and vowed to fight for Chinese, Malay, and Tamil languages to be listed as official languages.

Through Tan Chin Tuan, who represented the Chamber in the legislative assembly, the Chamber submitted a resolution to the Assembly calling for the abolishment of the language restriction. The resolution was in turn forwarded to the British government. At the same time, the Chamber rallied various local communities to sign a petition. Consequently, over 600 groups that represented about 140,000 residents and over 8,500 companies took part in the petitioning campaign.

While working to abolish the language restriction, the Chinese Chamber of Commerce also started a citizenship right movement for the multitude of residents who were not born here but had settled in Singapore and had allegiance towards Singapore.

With the local populace rallying to the movement, the Legislative Assembly of the Autonomous State of Singapore, established in 1959, abolished the language restrictions to allow the assemblymen to speak in English, Chinese, Malay, or Tamil. Furthermore, the hundreds of thousands of foreign-born residents who had taken root here were finally given Singapore citizenship.

The Chinese Chamber of Commerce played a key role in campaigning for citizenship rights and abolishing the language restrictions at the Assembly, and Tan Lark Sye was a stalwart supporter of the Chamber's efforts.

Fighting for a Level Playing Field in the Rubber Industry

In the colonial era, the rubber trade was controlled by the Western Rubber Traders' Association, which was set up by the British traders as a subsidiary of the London Rubber Company of England. The Association, which allowed local traders to be only affiliate members with no say over rubber trade, set rules which blatantly favoured the British traders. In the late 1940s, Tan Lark Sye and Lee Kong Chian formed their own rubber association, and demanded equal rights in the Western association. In the late 1960s, these two elders retired and passed the baton of leadership in the Rubber Association to Tan Eng Joo and Tan Keong Choon.

At the 21st AGM of the Hokkien Association in early September 1972, Tan Lark Sye asked his fellow clansmen to allow him to resign as chairman, a position he had held for more than 20 years. Several days later, on September 10, Tan had dinner with his friends at the Tanjong Rhu club. After he got home, he felt unwell, and the family doctor determined that he likely had a heart failure. He was sent to

General Hospital, and died within an hour, in the early morning of September 11, aged 76.

Universal Respect of Tan's Achievements

Throughout his life, Tan Lark Sye was guided by his belief of traditional Chinese values. He was generous, altruistic, and supported education, on which he spent a large part of his wealth. He followed the traditional chinese principle of quid proquo (especially regards to the society) strictly. He was loved by many, admired by most, and respected by all.

At his funeral, the faculty and students of Nanyang University draped his coffin with the University flag, and bore his coffin onto the hearse. Tan was laid to his final lasting rest at the Hokkien clan cemetery at Bukit Brown (popularly known as the Coffee Hill), as thousands lined the streets to bid him farewell.

Tan Lark Sye was survived by his sons Eng Hwah, Eng Ghee, Eng Chiong, Eng Bo, Eng Shun, Eng Sheng, Eng Han, Eng Xin, Eng Sen, and daughters Lan Ying and Xiu Ying. They carried on the family business or successfully struck out on their own. His nephew Tan Eng Jin took over Asia Life Insurance, while another nephew, Eng Joo, actively served the community. For many years he was chairman of the Rubber Trade Association and the Rubber Association of Singapore, Chairman and Permanent Director of the Chinese Chamber of Commerce, and the National Council of Forwarders.

Rest in Peace, Dear Uncle Tan Lark Sye, you have earned the rights to do so!

Appendix: Tan Lark Sye and the Tanjong Rhu Club

The well-known Tanjoing Rhu Club was the regular meeting place for Tan Lark Sye and his like-minded community leaders. Tanjong Rhu Club to Tan Lark Sye was very much like the Ee Hoe Hean Club to Tan Kah Kee.

Tan Lark Sye accumulated vast wealth during the Korean War in the early 1950s. In 1952 he chose a villa on the Tanjong Rhu beach to set up his Tanjong Rhu Club.

According to Loh Tze Wei, a former journalist who frequently went to the club to conduct interviews, the Club was a sprawling villa located near the Singapore Swimming Club, comprising of eight rooms on the first floor, three meeting rooms on the ground floor, and three courtyards. It was an ideal place to seek solace.

Soon Peng Yam, the chairman of Ee Hoe Hean Club in 1997, remembered how Tan Lark Sye regularly entertained his friends at the Tanjong Rhu Club.

Although Tan spoke only the Hokkien dialect, he got on extremely well with people from other dialect groups. His regular guests included Lee Kong Chian, Ko Teck Kin, Qiu Jixian, Tan Kong Piat and Lam Kwok Yan from the Hokkien group; Lien Ying Chow, Tan Siak Kew and Yap Pheng Gek from the Teochew group; Aw Boon Haw and Cheong Soon Chou from the Hakka group; and Foo Chee Fong from the Hainanese group.

Soon Peng Yam narrated that initially, both the Tanjong Rhu Club and the Ee Hoe Hean Club hosted weekly dinners on Saturdays. Tan Lark Sye then suggested that dinners at Tanjong Rhu Club be held on Sundays, so that acquaintances could meet more often.

Tanjong Rhu Club served several functions. It was a place to relax after work, by playing card games etc. It was also a place to discuss business. It was, more importantly, the gestation centre for the rich and powerful to strategise how to contribute to society, especially education. The plan to set up Nanyang University likely had its first roots there. From 1952 to 1963, (Tan Lark Sye resigned as Chairman of the Board of Nanyang University on September 25, 1963), Tanjong Rhu Club was regarded as the University's centre.

From 1953, many momentous events, like the naming of the University and the ways to raise fund, were decided at Tanjong Rhu Club. Volunteers wanting to raise fund usually met Tan Lark Sye at the Club.

When Tan Kah Kee left Singapore in 1949, Tan Lark Sye became the undisputed leader of the Hokkien clan. Important decisions relating to the Hokkien community were also frequently made at the Club.

Fittingly, Tan Lark Sye also had his last dinner (with some close friends) at the Club on September 10, 1972. He died in the wee hours on the next day in General Hospital.

After that, Tan Kong Piat took over as the Club chairman, when the club had about 200 members. But as members aged, and because of the government's intention to acquire the land, the remaining members had no choice but to dissolve the Club.

Soon Peng Yam added his personal speculation: the demise of the club had a lot to do with the demise of Tan Lark Sye, who was the magnet to attract members. Of course, another reason was that Soon Peng Yam had little time for the Club, as he was also the chairman of the Ee Hoe Hean Club.

Many journalists from the Chinese press would routinely go to the Club on Sunday evenings for informal press interviews. Most of them would address Tan as "Uncle Lark Sye." Although friendly and avuncular, Tan could be quite agitated if the journalists failed to publish what he wanted published.

Ko Teck Kin took over as club chairman in 1963 when Tan Lark Sye resigned as chairman of Nanyang University. From then on, the University's press conferences were no longer held at the Club, but at Ko Teck Kin's Kah Hing Shipping Company near the OCBC along North Canal Road.

According to Ong Chu Meng, one of the earliest Nanyang University alumni, Tan Lark Sye liked his young visitors, including Nanyang University undergraduates to be informal at the Club and treat him as a family elder.

Chapter 7

Tan Lark Sye and Nanyang University

Ng Kim Eng

The most important footprint left by Tan Lark Sye is the founding of Nanyang University. He was no doubt trying to emulate Tan Kah Kee's founding of the Xiamen University. But in some ways, Tan Lark Sye was even more remarkable because Nanyang University was the first Chinese university outside China.

The Background

The Chinese diaspora had one thing that was outstanding in the history of migration; wherever they went, they tried very hard to preserve their culture, and the most effective method was to set up institutions of learning to propagate the Chinese heritage.

By the 1950s, there were already 1,556 Chinese schools, enrolling 1.04 million students in Singapore and Malaya. In Malaya alone, there were 106 Chinese high schools, with more than 50,000 students. By 1957, even Sarawak had 13 high schools. Hence, there existed the necessary conditions for setting up a Chinese university for S.E. Asia.[1]

Before WW2, Chinese-stream students had no problems with tertiary education. They would go to China for further studies, and Chinese schools in S.E. Asia easily recruited teachers from China. With the founding of PRC (People's Republic of China) in 1949, all these changed. The colonial governments cut off almost all ties between S.E. Asian Chinese with China. Chinese education in Singapore and

Malaya therefore faced a new crisis. Worse than that, in order to cut off cultural ties between overseas Chinese and China, the colonial governments implemented policies to suppress Chinese education.

In 1950, when the University of Malaya was established, Chinese community leaders were hopeful that the University would set up a Faculty of Chinese. Tan Lark Sye generously donated $300,000 to the University, partly of this optimism. But the University seemed to be taking no action to set up such a Faculty, and the Chinese community was deeply disappointed.

The dream to set up a Chinese university was thus revived. Tan Lark Sye concluded that if the Chinese community failed to set up a Chinese university, their descendants would gradually become completely ignorant of their ancestry.

Lark Sye's Battle Cry Triggered a Tsunami

On January 16, 1953, at a meeting of the Hokkien Association, he analysed the situation Chinese education faced, and concluded that the founding of a Chinese university was a must.

He promised to sacrifice unreservedly for this noble cause, even to the extent of "going bankrupt." Tan's bold statement of intent roused a tremendous response from the Chinese masses, with virtually everyone joining the movement to build an ethnic bastion of culture.

The chairman of the Chinese Chamber of Commerce, Mr. Tan Siak Kew elaborated: "The Chinese in Singapore, unlike earlier immigrants, have taken roots here, and have no intention of returning to China. With a combined Chinese population of 2 to 3 million Chinese in Singapore and Malaya, the students attending Chinese schools in fact outnumber those attending English schools. We definitely need a Chinese university to churn out talents to serve the Chinese community. The difficulties for this project should not be insurmountable."

Other prominent community leaders, without exception, expressed their support for Tan Lark Sye.

Tan's only equal in the Chinese community, Lee Kong Chian, had just returned from a tour of the West in early 1953. He made the important point that the purpose of the proposed university was not to compete with the University of Malaya, but was to simply provide opportunities for non-English stream students to receive higher education.

Enthusiastic Response from Malaya

Chinese in Malaya were equally enthusiastic. The president of MCA (Malayan Chinese Association), Tan Cheng Lock, completely agreed with Tan Lark Sye's thinking, and pledged $10 million from the Malayan Chinese community. Many community leaders there backed their words by deeds, and donated generously towards the Nanyang University fund.

Backing from the Singapore and Malayan Chambers of Commerce

On January 21, 1954, the Singapore Chinese Chamber of Commerce held a meeting to express support for Tan Lark Sye's idea of joining forces with the Malayan Chinese. It elected a special team of representatives, comprising Tan Saik Kew, Ko Teck Kin, Lien Ying Chow, and Ng Aik Huan to attend the AGM of the Malayan Chinese Chamber of Commerce to be held on January 25, 1954, in Kuala Lumpur.

At the January 21 meeting, Tan Lark Sye gave greater details on the rationale for founding the Nanyang University. He said the Vice-Chancellor of the Malayan University had indicated that since his university would be conducing Chinese courses, there was no need for a Chinese university. But, Tan said he knew that the proposed Chinese courses were not formal courses, but sort of extra-curricular, conversational Chinese courses. The Malayan Chinese had donated generously towards Malayan University, but were disappointed after waiting 3 years in vain. He appealed to all sectors to help, including the Chinese press.

On January 25, 1954, the AGM of the Malayan Chinese Chamber of Commerce voted unanimously to support the founding of a Chinese university.

Encouraged by such overwhelming response, Tan Lark Sye announced, at a meeting in Tanjong Rhu Club on January 23, 1954, the detailed plans for Nanyang University. On behalf of the Hokkien Association, Tan also announced that the Association would donate 500 acres of land in the western part of Singapore. This idyllic piece of land by the seaside, later fondly named the Yunnan Garden, was ideal as a university campus.

Li Yurong, managing director of Nanyang Siang Pau, asked his staff and readers to give whole-hearted support for Nanyang University, and pledged to donate $100,000 towards the University fund every year for the next 10 years.

The founder of Sin Chew Jit Poh, Aw Boon Haw, was equally zealous.

On February 3, at a press conference in Tanjong Rhu Club, Tan Lark Sye expressed his confidence of the University's successful establishment, and explained that the funds required were not astronomical figures, and that we could all take heart from the success of Xiamen University.[2]

Tan Lark Sye Overcame Many Difficulties

But there were dissenting voices. First of them was Sir Sydney Caine, the Vice-chancellor of the University of Malaya, who opposed the establishment of Nanyang University on the ground that the University of Malaya was going to conduct courses in Chinese.

To counter opposing opinions like Caine's, Tan Cheng Lock specially came to Singapore to meet Tan Lark Sye for discussions. On January 28, Tan Cheng Lock and Caine had a radio debate, in which Tan Cheng Lock forcefully argued that the proposed university was the only way to provide opportunities for further studies for many high school graduates.

On February 12, the Singapore Chinese Chamber of Commerce invited 214 Chinese societies for a special conference, to discuss the formation of the University. Tan Lark Sye was chosen as chairman for the conference. The support for the university project was unanimous. Chinese newspapers outside Singapore and Malaya were also very supportive.

But the British government persisted in opposing the plan. On February 18, 1953, and again on February 22, Malcolm MacDonald, the British High Commissioner, summoned Tan Lark Sye and company and suggested that the Chinese community should wait for the University of Malaya to complete its expansion plan before establishing the Chinese University. But Tan and his team disagreed, and insisted that the establishment of Nanyang University was urgent.

On February 20, the University Planning Committee held its first meeting, and formally adopted the name Nanyang University. The committee was enlarged, and elected Tan Lark Sye as chairman, and the Chinese Chamber of Commerce as its secretary.

On March 24, Tan Lark Sye met Sir Carlson, the founder of the University of Malaya, who was on a trip to Malaya. Carlson had nothing to offer except repeating what MacDonald had said.

On March 26, the University applied to be "registered", not as a university, but as a private limited, in order to avoid any unforeseen complications.

On April 7, the University pronounced its manifesto:

(1) To provide high school leavers the opportunities for further studies;
(2) To train teachers for Chinese schools;
(3) To produce talents for Singapore (and Malaya);
(4) To provide talents for Singapore's growing economy.

The declaration also stated two other aims: to bridge Eastern and Western cultures; and to help promote local culture.

On May 5, 1953, University was at last registered as a legal entity as Nanyang University Limited.

Historic Malayan Conference

On May 19, at the second planning committee meeting, a Singapore Committee of the Nanyang University was formed, headed by Tan Lark Sye. Tan announced there and then that he would donate $5 million, comprising a first instalment of $2 million, plus $300,000 each year for the next 10 years.

Meanwhile, the entire Chinese community of Malaya was swept by the Support Nanyang University fever; almost everyone, regardless of social or financial status, contributed something. With increased confidence, Tan said, "In terms of wealth, I am only the third or fourth ranking in Singapore–Malaya. What makes me bold enough to initiate the establishment of Nanyang University is the strong will of the 3 million plus Chinese."

July 26 was a memorable day. On this day, the ground-breaking ceremony for the construction of the road to the campus was held. Tan said, "Let us sow the seeds of culture in this barren land, and its fruits will last as long as the Earth, the Moon, and the Sun."

The colonial government persisted in its obstructionism. But at last, under the pressure of public opinion, the government gave way and approved Nanyang University's building plan, and exempted the donations it received from taxes. Soon, the Malayan government did likewise.

Soon after this, on August 5, all regional Nanyang University committees in Singapore and Malaya held a representatives' conference, to express support for the university. The conference elected Tan Lark Sye as chairman, who reiterated that the driving force for the establishment of the university was not him, but the masses. He also said that there were many who were richer than him, and appealed to all to help the cause.

The conference also approved the constitution of the university, and decided to enlarge its structure: number of general members increased from 250, to 2,500, and number of executive committee members from 25 to 250.

This conference greatly increased the unity between the Singapore and Malayan Chinese communities. At the same time, it helped spread the message to areas beyond Singapore–Malaya, like North Borneo and beyond, where the Chinese communities became just as zealous in supporting Nanyang University.

Contribution Fever

In 1954, when the construction of the campus began in earnest, a spectacular never-seen-before phenomenon occurred. The entire

Chinese communities in Singapore and Malaya seemed to be in a frenzy to contribute to the success of Nanyang University. The two main Chinese newspapers in Singapore alone collected more than $280,000 from their readers in one year. More outstanding of these efforts were the Basket Ball Competition in Malaya (more than $230,000) and stage plays by High school students (more than $60,000). What was really touching were people who were normally regarded as belonging to the lower social classes like trishaw riders, taxi drivers, and dance hostesses, all put aside their sweat, toil, and tear to contribute money for the University.

Among the rich, those who made significant contributions included Aw Boon Haw, Lee Kong Chian, Lien Ying Chow, and Loke Wan Toh. And those rich and powerful from beyond Singapore would not be left on the bench too. From Penang, Lin Liandeng contributed $500,000 and Liu Yushui gave $250,000.

Plaques, or other items of remembrance, were made to commemorate these acts of largess. What was most unforgettable was perhaps the big clock donated by the Trishaw Riders Association.

Lin Yutang Affair

While Nanyang University was being constructed, its board was busy head-hunting, hoping to find a suitable candidate to run the university. After failing to recruit Hu Shi and Mei Yiqi, the University got Lin Yutang to agree to be the inaugural president of the university. Dr. Lin was a famous scholar, and expectations were high. On October 2, 1954, Lin arrived in Singapore to take up the appointment. But immediately Lin made some public statements which were both puzzling and highly politicised.

On December 16, some of the better-known high schools in Singapore sent a joint letter to Tan Lark Sye and Lin Yutang, asking them to find solutions to two urgent issues: the further studies for high school graduates, and the crunch in qualified teaching staff for high schools. On December 12, Lin Yutang invited the school principals to a meeting. It was then decided that the University would conduct preparatory classes for university entrance. On February 1,

1955, applications were opened and examinations were held simultaneously in Singapore, Kuala Lumpur, Ipoh, and Penang. 497 students were successful, and the three-month course would begin on March 14.

Before the classes could commence, Lin and the University became bitterly antagonised in what would later be known as the Lin Yutang Affair. It all started with Lin's demands for excessive salaries and allowances, and an immediate sum of $20 million as budget for expenditure, without any supervision or concurrence of the Board.

To those who cared for Nanyang University, it was a scandal. Public opinions were expressed, condemning Lin's extravagance. Lin threatened to take the matter to the courts, and tried to engage the legal service of David Marshall, one of the most prominent lawyers in Singapore. Marshall declined, but offered his service to mediate.

By March 25, the Singapore committee of the Nanyang University sent a team of authorised representatives headed by Li Juncheng to discuss with Lin Yutang to find a solution. By April 3, Lin accepted a severance payment of $300,000, paid by Tan Lark Sye personally, as settlement.

On April 7, a 7-men selection committee was formed to appoint staff to run the University, and conduct the Pre-university courses.

But the matter did not rest there. Lin flew to France, where he made insulting comments on the Chinese education of Singapore–Malaya. Public opinions almost unanimously expressed disgust and outrage. Even the Chinese newspapers in New York criticised Lin, saying that the root cause of the trouble was Lin's nepotism and cronyism, and Lin had disgraced himself through this affair.

Undaunted, Tan Lark Sye issued his plans for the pre-university classes on April 23, 1955. The principals of Chinese High School and Zhongzheng High School were drafted to help run the courses.

On August 12, chief minister David Marshall, accompanied by education minister Chew Swee Kee, and labour minister Lim Yew Hock, went to visit the University. Marshall was impressed by the edifices, and gave the University his blessings, confident that it would become one of the best universities in S.E. Asia. On August 22, the British colonial secretary was invited to see the University, still under construction. The Secretary also wished the University well.

Opening of the University in Midst of Difficulties

By 1956, the University was busy preparing for opening. A team of academics was appointed. Entrance examinations were held in Singapore, Kuala Lumpur, and Penang. On March 3, examination results were announced and 330 students were admitted.

On March 3, an administrative committee was formed, which would represent the University in external affairs, and would internally supervise university administration, and whose chairman would be the president of the University. The members were appointed by Tan Lark Sye, for one year. Soon, the University recruited many well-known scholars to join the teaching staff.[3]

On March 15, 1956, the University was at last officially opened. For the first time, a complete range of education in Chinese became available in S.E. Asia. When the University flag was raised, the crowd chanted "Long live Nantah!" The University received many greetings from all quarters, including one from the chief minister David Marshall. Tan Lark Sye declared, "This is the finest hour of the overseas Chinese for them to rely on their own resources to overcome all difficulties and built a University."

Formal classes began on March 30, with 239 students in Faculty of Arts, 256 in Science, and 89 in Commerce, totalling 584. This date would subsequently become the University Anniversary.

Public opinions began to swing. Those initially opposed to the establishment of the University, including some political parties, gradually became more supportive. The ruling Labour Front urged the government to recognise Nanyang University degrees.

On March 30, 1958, Nanyang University held a grand ceremony to mark the completion of the campus construction, with Singapore governor Sir William Goode as guest of honour. The confluence of more than 100,000 well-wishers and spectators caused massive traffic jams, and some had to walk 10 kilometres to reach Yunnan Garden.

All appeared well on the surface. But dark clouds were looming, over the recognition of Nanyang University degrees and the University's academic standards.

Controversy of the Assessment Committee's Reports

In January 1959, Nanyang University and the Singapore government agreed to form a high-powered committee, comprising well-known university administrators and academics from overseas to assess the academic standards of Nanyang University, to be headed by vice-Chancellor S.L Prescott of University of Western Australia.

On March 4, the Nanyang University Act was passed by the Singapore legislature. But the recognition of its degrees was not discussed.

On July 22, the Prescott Report was published. It was quite critical of Nanyang University's administration. The committee took only one month to complete its report, and had resorted to secret polling to get its information. This caused many Nanyang University supporters to doubt the report's reliability, and the government's intention in appointing the committee.[4]

Singapore's minister for education, Yong Nyuk Lin, then appointed a second committee, headed by Dr. Gwee Ah Leng and comprised of mainly highly regarded local intellectuals, to review the report of the Prescott Committee.

On January 11, 1960, the Singapore committee of the Nanyang University held its first meeting, and Tan Lark Sye announced the appointment of Dr. Zhuang Zhulin as the university president, and other key appointments.

On February 8, finance minister Goh Keng Swee announced that the government would employ some of the first batch of Nanyang University graduates. As regards future batches, it would depend on the progress of the restructuring of the University.

On February 9, the Gwee Ah Leng committee published its report. It more or less reiterated the main points of the Prescott Report. The Nanyang University supporters expressed their unease. An editorial of the Sin Chew Jit Poh said, "The main emphasis of the Gwee Ah Leng Report is to reform Nanyang University on the model of University of Malaya. This completely ignores the raison d'etre of the University, and therefore the Committee has prescribed a completely wrong medicine to improve the University's health. And it also misleads the public to believe that the government intends to merge it with the University of Malaya. The second error zone is its recommendation on the medium of instruction, forgetting that the main objective of establishment of the University was to enable Chinese high school leavers to further their studies."[5]

On February 10, education minister Yong Nyuk Lin stated in the Legislative Assembly that the government in principle accepted the Gwee Ah Leng Report. On February 10, Yong held a meeting with Tan Lark Sye and 27 members of the Nanyang University's executive committee.

Nanyang University Graduates Served Their Communities

On April 2, 1960, the first graduation ceremony was held, with 437 students graduating. That day large crowds again flocked to the campus. In his speech Tan Lark Sye said, "Judging from the continual support from the communities in Singapore and Malaya, and the increasing numbers of enrollment, it is obvious that the establishment of the University satisfies the communities' needs, and the founders were therefore vindicated."

Most of the first batch of graduates joined the teaching profession, thus fulfilling one of the initial aims of the University. But differences remained between the University and the government. On May 4, the University agreed with the government to form a special liaison committee to resolve the matter, but they could not agree on the composition of the committee.

On November 14, the second Final Examinations were held, and external examiners from Taiwan, Hong Kong, and the United States were invited to oversee it.

On March 30, 1961, a graduation ceremony was held for the second batch of graduates of 344. At the ceremony, education minister Yong acknowledged the good work done by the first batch of graduates, and expressed his hope that the good work would continue.

On July 14, 1962, the first governing Board was formed in accordance with the Nanyang University Act. One member from Singapore and one from each of the 11 Malayan states were appointed to the board, together with three members nominated by the government, two members nominated by the University, and two members nominated by the Alumni Association. Tan Lark Sye was elected as chairman.

From 1960 to 1962, little progress was made, due to disagreement over the composition of the Board. On September 25, 1963, Tan Lark Sye resigned as chairman of the Board, but his care and concern for the University was not reduced by an iota.

Realising Tan Lark Sye's Aims

The graduates of Nanyang University did not let their Alma Mater down all theses years, but brought glory upon it. They served in education, commerce and industry, and government agencies. The achievement of the University has exceeded what was originally expected of it. They served not only S.E. Asia, but the whole world.

When Tan Lark Sye died on September 11, 1972, countless people mourned his death. On September 14, 1972, the University board announced that it would erect a bronze statue of Tan in the University campus.

Finally, at the erection ceremony on June 15, 1974, the Tan family announced that it would donate $500,000 to fund the Tan Lark Sye scholarship.

Appendix: Tan Lark Sye and the Hokkien Huay Kuan (Association)

Tan Lark Sye was very much involved in the affairs of Hokkien Association. He was chairman for 11 terms, or 22 years, from 1950 to 1972. During this period, the Association contributed a lot to social welfare and education in Singapore.

Purchasing property for the Hokkien Association

In 1952, Tan Lark Sye purchased a 900-acre plot of land in Jurong, called Yunnan Garden, on behalf of the Hokkien Association. On January 23, 1953, Tan Lark Sye, as chairman of the Association, donated 500 acres of Yunnan Garden to be used as the Nanyang University campus. In April 1960, the government requisitioned over 32 acres of old cemetery land in Tiong Bahru Road owned by the Association, and in September 1962, the government requisitioned another 18 acres of the Association's land. The Association received $630,000 as compensation, of which $600,000 was donated to the Nanyang University as building fund.

In 1964, Tan Lark Sye purchased 391 acres of land in Mandai Garden on behalf of the Association for $260,000. In the same year, he purchased another 131 acres in Sembawang for $520,000. The income derived from these lands after they were developed paid for the maintenance, expansion, and relocation of the five schools set up by the Association: Tao Nan School, Ai Tong School, Chong Hock School, Nan Chiau School, and Kong Hwa School. The Association also paid the salaries of the teachers, some of whom were recruited from China.[6]

In August 1962, the government requisitioned over 50 acres of old cemetery land owned by the Association in Leng Kee Hill for $370,000. In March 1966, another 3 acres of open land opposite the Leng Kee plot was requisitioned for $60,000. In April 1966, 45 acres in Yunnan Garden was requisitioned for $68,000.[7]

Construction of the Hokkien Huay Kuan building

In 1945, when the Hokkien Association decided to construct a new 6-storey building, Tan Lark Sye and Lee Kong Chian donated $200,000 each towards the building fund. The new building, which was where the Chinese opera (wayang) stage was usually set up (opposite the Thian Hock Keng Temple, along Telok Ayer Street), was completed in 1955. It served as the Association's office, and also housed two affiliated schools, Chong Hock Girls' School and Ai Tong School. The auditorium was used as a centre for social activities.

In view of the serious shortage of school places in the 1950s, Tan Lark Sye spearheaded a move to set up Kong Hwa School in May 1953, increasing the number of affiliated schools from 4 to 5.

In 1965, Tan Lark Sye proposed setting up a $3 million charity fund, whose returns would be used for charity and education, including scholarships and bursaries. The Association passed a resolution in August 1969, adopting Tan Lark Sye's plan to develop 400 acres of Yunnan Garden to build 173 residential units.

Hokkien Association also organised mass weddings, aided by Aihua Music Society, at the Great World Amusement Park. Seventeen such ceremonies were held during Tan Lark Sye's tenure, from 1956 to 1960, when the Women's Charter was passed.

During Tan Lark Sye's tenure, Hokkien Association went beyond dialect boundaries to invite people from all of Fujian Province, like Fuzhou, Xinghua, Zhangzhou, Quanzhou, Yongchun and Hakka people to join the Association, thus making it a truly an association of the Fujian Province.[8]

The development of Tao Nan School

Tao Nan School, the oldest of the 5 Hokkien Association schools, was set up on November 8, 1906, by over 100 Fujian merchants, and was initially named Dao Nan Xue Tang. After a meeting at Thian Hock Keng, the Hokkien Association decided to set up the school at Siam House, the residence of Tan Kim Ching, along North Bridge Road (formerly the Bata shoe factory). Forty directors were elected by the donors, with Wu Shouzhen as the head of management of the school, and Ma Zhengxiang as its principal. Classes were conducted in the Hokkien dialect.

In 1910, sugar tycoon Oei Tiong Ham donated $10,000 to purchase a plot of land along Armenian Street to be the school's permanent site. In the following year, Tan Kah Kee took over the school management, and raised $50,000 to build the school. The new school was completed by March 1912, and renamed Tao Nan School. It became the first school in Singapore to use Mandarin as medium of instruction. In 1929, Hokkien Association took over the school.

In autumn 1935, Pan Guoqu (Pan Shou) became the principal, and the school received a substantial subsidy from the government. The school underwent renovation and rejuvenation, and student enrolment swelled. In 1940, Pan left to join Chung Hwa Hua Nan School in Muar. Zhang Shu took over as principal. Before long, war broke out, the school was destroyed and closed down.

After the war, Hokkien Association rushed to rebuild the school. At that time Tan Kah Kee was chairman of the Association, and Lee Chin Tiam the director of education. Lin Juren was appointed the new principal, who championed the life education ideology of Tao Xingzhi.

Tan Lark Sye took over as the Association's chairman in 1949. The association's director for education, Huang Fukang, formed a special joint committee called Educational Promotion Committee. It comprised all teaching staff of the four affiliated schools, 10 student representatives, and two alumni members from each of the four affiliated schools. The inaugural meeting of the committee was held in Nan Chiau High School.

At the end of 1950, Lin Juren stepped down as principal, and was succeeded by Huang Xiaoyun. In 1952, when Zeng Zhisheng became the Association's director of education, he pushed for the expansion of the affiliated schools. At the end of 1958, Huang Xiaoyun resigned to return to China, and Hong Changshu took over as principal.

In 1971, Hong Changshu retired, and Zheng Kaiguo succeeded him. Since then, student enrolment declined steadily due to urban redevelopment. In January 1977, Zhang Kaiguo died of heart attack, and senior teacher Chen Yuling succeeded him.

The school premises were deemed to be outdated for modern education, and the Hokkien Association decided to build a new school in Marine Parade. By end of 1981, the new Tao Nan School was completed. In early 1982, Tao Nan School officially moved to Marine Parade.

The development of Ai Tong School

Ai Tong School, founded on October 12, 1912, was the second oldest affiliated school. It started in the Methodist Church in Boon Tat Street (popularly called Japan Street,) and ran classes there until 1916, when the school was relocated to an old house at 209 Telok Ayer Street which it bought over. Later, the school ran into financial difficulties, and was taken over by the Hokkien Association.

After the war, the school expanded to meet demand, by renting the old Gan Eng Seng School building along Cecil Street to run it as a branch school. The total student enrolment jumped from 470 to 1,600 within one year.

The environment around Ai Tong School was not conducive for learning, with abundant gambling dens around. The school principal, Ye Fanfeng, decided to go alone to meet one of the gangster chiefs.

When they met, the gangster chief, named Liao, asked, "Whose backing do you have to be the principal of Ai Tong School?" Ye answered, "Hokkien Association is my backer, and Uncle Lark Sye is my boss." Liao immediately became very respectful, and promised to solve the problem.

The next day, when Ye arrived in the vicinity of the school, he saw that all the gambling dens were gone.[9]

When the Hokkien Association Building was completed in 1954, Ai Tong School and Chong Hock Girls' School moved in at the same time. The old campus of the Ai Tong School became the branch school of Chong Hock Girls' School, while the branch school of Ai Tong School remained.

When both San Shui and Tong Hua Schools were closed down in 1961, all the teachers and students were absorbed into Ai Tong School, swelling its student population to 2,360. In 1962, the government stopped renting out the branch school campus, so a portion of the students were transferred to Yang Zheng School while the rest were transferred to Umar Pulawar Tamil School at Maxwell Road. It was then when Ai Tong School began to shrink.

During the 1970s, due to urban redevelopment, student population in urban schools declined sharply. Because of this the Hokkien Association began building a new Ai Tong School at Ang Mo Kio Avenue 3. In 1980, Ai Tong School moved to Ang Mo Kio. Due to changes in environment, the school moved yet again in July 1992 to Bright Hill Drive, where it was headed by principal Ting Beng Chin.

The development of Chongfu Primary School

The third affiliated school, Chongfu School, was originally named Chong Hock Girls' School, established on April 16, 1915. It was the first school set up directly by the Hokkien Association. It initially used the Chongwen Ge building (built in 1849, next to the Thian Hock Keng Temple) as school. Soon, Chongwen Ge was expanded till it is next to the old Hokkien Association building (built in 1913.)

Chong Hock Girls' School was founded by Wang Huiyi, then Director of Education of the Hokkien Association. He believed that girls should be educated, just like boys. So he founded Singapore's first all-girls school, in the heart of Telok Ayer, which had the densest Chinese population. The teaching medium was Hokkien, and the first principal was Madam Lin Shuqin.

In 1930 the school was shifted to Stanley Street, which was behind the wayang stage across the road from Thian Hock Keng Temple. In the same year, Tan Kah Kee became the Association president. He accepted the school as belonging to the Association, and engaged Wu Dexian as the school's second principal, and changed the teaching medium to Mandarin. In 1931, a kindergarten section was added to the school.

In 1934, when principal Wu resigned, Huang Jing acted as principal, until Lin Fanglan took over as the the third principal. The school flourished under Lin's leadership. Lin resigned in 1940, and an interim committee took over the running of the school. In early 1941, Lim Boh Seng, then Director of Education of the Association, appointed Huang Huizhen as the fourth principal, who held that position until the fall of Singapore in WW2.

A month after the WW2 ended, Chong Hock School was restarted, with Shi Peirong as its fifth principal. The student enrolment increased to more than 1,000. In 1949, the school began to accept boys who were brothers of girl students. In 1951, Li Peilan became the sixth principal. By 1953, Chong Hock became a full co-education school.

During the period when Tan Lark Sye was the Association chairman, the school building at Stanley Street was torn down to make way for the Association building. When the building was completed in 1956, Chong Hock moved into its new premises next to the new Association building, together with Ai Tong School. Ai Tong's old school building at the corner of Amoy Street became a branch of Chong Hock Girls' to cater for increasing student population. By 1956, the student population at Chong Hock reached 2,400, and became one of the largest primary schools in Singapore.

In 1966, principal Li retired, and Chen Shujuan took over as the seventh principal. In 1978, the land of the branch school was acquired by the government, and the school had to close. The students there were integrated into the main school. In 1981, the school was renamed Chongfu Primary School, and principal Chen retired in the same year.

In November 1981, Chong Sui Tiam was appointed as the eighth principal, and the school was relocated to its new campus in Yishun New Town.

The development of Nan Chiau High School

Nan Chiau High School was initially set up as Nan Chiau Girls' High School in March 1947 at 46 Kim Yam Road. It was the Association's only high school. It also had a primary school section.

Nan Chiau High School started as Nan Chiau Teachers' Training School by Tan Kah Kee in 1941. It was built on a plot of land with mansion donated by Lee Kong Chian. Zhuang Guizhang was its inaugural principal. The school ceased operations during the Japanese occupation. After the war, the Association decided not to restart the Nan Chiau Teachers' Training College, but convert it to Nan Chiau Girls' High School in 1947, with initial enrolment of 900, its first principal was Yang Zhenli.

In 1951, Yang resigned and Qiu Rentuan took over. A boarding school was set up for the girls. The student population gradually increased to 1,300 in 1960. In July, Ngo Soo Kwee acted as principal upon principal Qiu's death.

In 1961, Lin Fanglan took over as principal and was responsible for starting afternoon session. In 1962, student population increased to beyond 2,000, and Sim Boon Peng was appointed its vice-principal. In 1966, Sim was appointed Director of People's Association, and Zhao Chengbang took over as vice-principal.

In 1965, Hokkien Association, with Tan Lark Sye as chairman, spent $2 million to rebuild Nan Chiau. During the rebuilding, Nan Chiau operated out of a temporary campus in Guillemard Road for more than four years.

In 1968, Principal Lin Fanglan retired, and in January 1969 Kau Ah Suo became principal. In May that year, the new school building was completed, and the high school section moved back to the new campus at Kim Yam Road. By the end of 1969, the rebuilding project was completed, and by now Nan Chiau had become a modern high school with full facilities.

By 1974, the number of students swelled to 2,600, and the Hokkien Association spent a further $300,000 in 1976 to extend the school building.

In 1980, vice-principal Zhao retired and Zhang Weixuan took over. In May 1983, Nan Chiau took the advice of the Ministry of Education, and converted itself into a co-education school in 1984. It was renamed Nan Chiau High School. In February 1985, Zhang Weixuan resigned and Chan Mee Leen took over as vice-principal.

In 1986, the school added a woodwork and metalwork workshop to its campus. In November that year, principal Kau Ah Suo retired, and Chen Mee Leen oversaw the running of the school. In 1988, Lee Mianyan took over as vice-principal cum acting principal. In 1989, Lee Mianyan was redeployed to the Ministry, and Su Wei Cher took over as principal.

The development of Kong Hwa School

Kong Hwa School was founded during Tan Lark Sye's chairmanship of Hokkien Association, increasing the number of affiliated schools from four to five.

Kong Hwa School was founded in May 1953 along Guillemard Road to provide education for the Geylang area. At first it was intended to name it Kong Chian School in honour of Lee Kong Chian for his contribution to education. But when Lee heard about the intention, he strongly opposed it, and the Association finally decided to name it Kong Hwa School.

The school had the best of facilities. Moreover, due to its central location, it quickly became a very popular school, and student enrolment soon rose to 1,700 from 400.

The first principal, Lau Siu Ching, graduated from Jimei Normal School, and was an experienced teacher and school principal. He laid strong foundations for the school, but resigned in the autumn of 1960. The Association then deployed Ngo Soo Kwee, acting principal of Nan Chiau Girls' High, to take over as principal. Under principal Ngo's charge, the school enrolment reached 2,500.

To develop the school further, the Association spent $90,000 to acquire a neighbouring plot of land to house a new high school section. Later, while Nan Chiau Girls' High underwent reconstruction, its students moved into the new wing to continue their classes.

In 1959, after the new campus of Nan Chiau was completed, the Association reached an agreement with Chung Cheng High School to swap Nan Chiau's new campus in Guillemard Road with the branch campus of Chung Cheng High School in Kim Yam Road.

In 1970, Principal Ngo Soo Kwee resigned, and Ng Soh Beng took up the post until his resignation in 1986. In 1988, Lam Kam Choon took over as principal. After principal Lam retired in 1991, Pang Hong Tin took over as principal.[10]

At a meeting of the Hokkien Association held in 1972, in which Tan Lark Sye tendered his resignation as chairman, he reported that during his last few years of office, the Association had donated a total of more than $4 million to Nanyang University, Chong Cheng High School, National Junior College, Kong Hwa School, and Nan Chiau High School. But the Association had built up sufficient financial resources, for even greater things to come.

Endnotes

1. Lin Yunhi 林运辉，Zhang Yinglong 张应龙，*History of Overseas Chinese in Singapore and Malaysia* <<新加坡马来西亚华侨史>>，广东高等教育出版社，1991

2. *History of Nanyang University's Founding*,《南洋大学创校史》，新加坡南洋文化出版社，1961

3. 《南洋大学史料汇编》，马来亚南洋大学校友会，1990年

4. 古鸿廷,《东南亚华侨的认同问题》，台湾联经出版社，1994

5. *Sin Chew Jit Poh*, 2 June 1960

6. *Inaugural Issue of Chuan Deng Newsletter*, Singapore Hokkien Huay Kuan, December 1992

7. Chen Weilong, *Brief Biographies of Famous Chinese in Southeast Asia*, Nanyang Society, October 1977

8. *The Winds from Fujian Cross to the South,* Singapore Hokkien Huay Kuan, 10 February 1990

9. Ye Fangfeng, *15 Years of Wind and Rain*, Seng Yew Book Store, December 1996

10. *A Short Introduction to the Singapore Hokkien Huay Kuan*, Singapore Hokkien Huay Kuan, 1 March 1995

Chapter 8

A Chronology of Tan Lark Sye's Life

Tan Yam Seng

One year old in 1897	On June 7, 1897 (in the 23rd year of the reign of Emperor Guangxu), Tan Lark Sye was born in Jimei Village, Tong'an County of Fujian Province (presently under the jurisdiction of Xiamen City) in China, which was also the birthplace of Tan Kah Kee.
Born in Jimei Village	Tan's family was poor, making a living on farming and fishing. Tan Lark Sye was the sixth of seven sons by his father Tan Kee Peck. The seven sons, from the eldest to the youngest, were Boon Ek, Boon Ching, Boon Kue, Ko Dow, Boon Choo, Lark Sye, and Boon Chiang.
	Lark Sye was born at a time when China was facing trouble at home and aggression from abroad, which had weakened the country and impoverished the people. However, it was also the dawn of the National Revolution.
	Amoi (Xiamen), a city near Tan's hometown, was appointed as one of the Five Treaty Ports when Hong Kong was ceded to Great Britain during the Opium War in 1840.

The Sino–Japanese War of 1894–1895	Two years before he was born, in 1895, the Qing Dynasty suffered a humiliating defeat in the Sino–Japanese War of 1894–1895 and was forced to sign the Treaty of Shimonoseki, under which Taiwan was ceded to Japan.
	In the same year, a group of activists led by Kang Youwei submitted a Joint Petition of Imperial Examination Candidates to the Emperor, urging the Imperial court to initiate political reform.
Two years old in 1898 Political Reform	Upon accepting the reform proposal by Kang Youwei, Liang Qichao and others, Guangxu Emperor carried out the Reform Movement of 1898 (Wuxu Reform) and the Hundred Days of Reform, which lasted from June 11 to September 21. However, Empress Dowager Cixi seized power and Emperor Guangxu was put under house arrest, while the "Six Gentlemen of the Hundred Day's Reform", including Tan Sitong, were killed.
	In the same year, the Boxers staged an uprising in Shandong.
Four years old in 1900	The anti-foreigner movement of the Boxers reached its climax.
The Eight-Power Allied Forces	The Eight-Power Allied Forces from Great Britain, Japan, Russia, France, the United States, Germany, Italy and Austria–Hungary invaded China and captured Beijing and Tianjin. The Qing Government was forced to sign the Treaty of 1901, under which 450 million taels of silver were paid to the invaders as indemnity and the foreign countries were allowed to base their troops in the Embassy District in Beijing.

Six years old in 1902 Orphaned	Tan Lark Sye's father Tan Kee Peck and mother Mdm. Lim died on the same day of a plague. Soon after, eldest brother Boon Ek and wife also succumbed to the plague. The family was plunged into even deeper poverty.
Nine years old in 1905 Chinese United League by Sun Yat-sen Fifteen years old in 1911	In August, Sun Yat-sen organised the Chinese United League and advocated the Three People Principles Doctrine. Before that, in July, the Qing Government abolished the imperial examination system and started running modern schools in China. In April, the Second Guangzhou Uprising (Yellow Flower Mound Revolt) led by Sun Yat-sen and Huang Xing failed. 72 revolutionaries were killed.
Birth of Republic of China	In October, the Wuchang Uprising in Hubei succeeded, and the Hubei Military Government was established. The country was officially named "The Republic of China". This event is historically known as the Xinhai Revolution. On December 17, Sun Yat-sen was elected the first provisional President of the Republic of China by representatives from 17 provinces.
Sixteen years old in 1912 Yuan Shikai came to power.	On February 12, Emperor Xuantong of the Qing Dynasty announced his abdication, signifying the demise of the Qing Dynasty. On March 10, Sun Yat-sen abdicated in order to ally the northern warlords. Yuan Shikai became the provisional President of Republic of China in Beijing. During the following 15 years, the northern warlords never ceased fighting for supreme power.

Seventeen years old in 1913	In 1913, Jimei Primary School, sponsored by Tan Kah Kee, was founded and started accepting students the same year.
Studied in Jimei Primary School	Among the seven brothers, only Tan Lark Sye and his third brother Tan Boon Kue and seventh brother Tan Boon Chiang were able to study in Jimei Primary School for free. Later, Tan Boon Kue quitted school because he had to support the family.
	Since Tan's big family owned a small farmland, it was difficult for them to eke out a living. Therefore, they decided to send one brother to seek opportunities abroad. At that time, the second brother was already married, so they decided that third brother Tan Boon Kue should venture abroad to give it a try.
Tan Boon Kue coming south	On his arrival at Singapore, Tan Boon Kue firstly worked on a cargo ferry boat owned by one of his town fellows. Unfortunately, the ship sank in an accident. Tan Boon Kue then went to work in Tan Kah Kee's pineapple factory. He learnt on the job how to do paperwork and bookkeeping. Later he was promoted to be a secretary, then a manager. After that, Tan Kah Kee sent him to manage a rubber plantation in Malaya. Soon after, fourth brother Ko Dow, and then fifth brother Boon Choo, came south to join Boon Kue in Tan Kah Kee's company.
	In March, 1913, Yuan Shikai assassinated Song Jiaoren and started to suppress the Kuomintang (KMT).

Eighteen years old in 1914 Outbreak of the First World War	On July 28, the First World War broke out between the two opposing sides — the Central Powers (German, Austria–Hungary and Bulgaria) and the Allied Powers of more than ten countries, including Great Britain, France, Russia, Italy, and the United States. German and Austria–Hungary provoked the war none other than to expand their territories, to capture resources and markets, and to realise a reign of racialism and hegemonism. In September, Japan used a declaration of war against German as a pretext to send troops to seize Germany's assets in Shandong, China, wrestling over control of the Jiaozhou-Ji'nan Railway and Qingdao.
Nineteen years old in 1915 The Twenty-one Demands	In January, Japan issued the "Twenty-one Demands" to Yuan Shikai in exchange for Japan's support of him being the emperor. Most of the Demands were readily accepted.
Twenty years old in 1916 Tan Lark Sye went abroad.	In 1916, following his three elder brothers, Tan Lark Sye came over to Singapore to make a living, as well as seventh brother Boon Chiang. Tan Lark Sye once talked about his first arrival at Singapore: The first thing he did was to pay respect to Tan Kah Kee and his brother Jingxian. Then he was sent to work in the rubber plantation of Khiam Aik (Qianyi) Company in Malaya. Lark Sye's diligence was recognised by Tan Kah Kee and half a year later, he was made a supervisor in a rubber

	factory in Singapore. Lark Sye's usual attire at work was only a pair of wooden clogs and a pair of shorts. Initially, he earned 4 straits dollars every month, with free meals and accommodation provided. He was a frugal person, spending only about 1 straits dollars every month and saving the rest. Later he was transferred to work in Tan Kah Kee's office to assist in the rubber trading business.
Twenty one years old in 1917	At the time when Tan Lark Sye arrived, Singapore had been governed by Great Britain for 97 years ever since Sir Thomas Stamford Raffles arrived in 1819 and established it as a trading port. The Chinese population then was about 250,000. Singapore had become an entrepôt when Lark Sye arrived, functioning as the distribution centre for cotton textiles and industrial products from Great Britain; rubber, tin, spices and rice from Southeast Asia; and raw silk, tea leaves and porcelain ware from China.
Rubber industry in Singapore	The rubber industry had, by then, become a major component in the economy of Singapore and Malaya. In Singapore, Chinese businessmen such as Tan Kah Kee and Lim Nee Soon owned 30 rubber factories at that time. After 1900, modern Chinese primary schools were started in Singapore. There were 15 Chinese schools then, including Ying Xin, Qifa, Yeung Cheng, Tao Nan, Yuying, and Chung Hua Girl's School.
Chinese High School	In 1918, The Chinese High School was founded by Tan Kah Kee and various Chinese community leaders.

Twenty-two years old in 1918 End of the First World War	On November 11, Germany was defeated and the First World War ended. About 20 million soldiers and civilians were killed in the war. The military spending was about US$200 billion, while property damages amounted to over US$150 billion.
Twenty three years old in 1919	On January 18, the Allied victors held a peace conference in Paris to set down the peace terms for Germany. It was decided at the Paris Peace Conference that the German assets in Shandong, China were transferred to Japan.
The May Fourth Movement	On May 4, 1919, the May Fourth Movement broke out with students demonstration in Beijing, shouting slogans such as "Fight for sovereignty abroad, punish the national traitors at home", "Abolish the Twenty-One Demands", "Return Qingdao". The movement soon spread across the country and forced the government of the Northern Warlords to refuse endorsing the Paris Peace Treaty. In October, Sun Yat-sen reorganised the Chinese Revolutionary Party into the Kuomintang of China.
Twenty five years old in 1921 Lark Sye went back to get married in his hometown	Tan Lark Sye went back to get married in his hometown. After the wedding, he took his wife to live in Singapore and continued his work in Tan Kah Kee's company. The Chinese Communist Party was founded at the first representative conference in Shanghai held from July 23 to 31. Mao Zedong was among those who attended the conference. From then on, China's political world would witness the struggle between the Kuomintang and the Communist Party.

Twenty seven years old in 1923	Tan Lark Sye and his brother were passionate learners. From their stint at Tan Kah Kee's rubber plantations and factories, they had learnt the rope of business skills in rubber tapping, rubber sheets production, management of rubber plantations, processing technology, rubber sheet grading, and the organisation and management of a rubber factory.
Starting their own business	In the same year, Tan and his brothers set up the Lian Hoe Rubber Company. They hired a retired manager to take care of the business but they lost money. Seventh brother Tan Boon Chiang quitted his job to take charge of the company. However, there was not much improvement. Tan Lark Sye and Tan Boon Kuek also quitted their job to run Lian Hoe Rubber Company. At the same time, fourth brother Ko Dow went into a joint investment with his friends and started a barge freighting and postal business.
Twenty nine years old in 1925	This was a good year for the rubber market, with prices reaching 200 straits dollars per picul ($1.80 straits dollars per pound).
Establishment of Aik Hoe Rubber Company	Lark Sye and his third brother Boon Kue rode on the market uptrend and set up Aik Hoe Rubber Company, with Lark Sye as the general manager. They pushed hard to develop their rubber business. Within ten years, the company became one of the top 10 rubber businesses in Singapore and Malaya. In addition to Aik Hoe, the Tan brothers subsequently set up Hiap Hoe Rubber Co. Ltd, Asia United Company, and Tan Yung Ek Private Co. Ltd.

Sun Yat-sen passed away	On March 12, Sun Yat-sen, the leader of the Chinese revolution, passed away. In July, the Guangdong Revolutionary Government was reorganised into the National Government of the Republic of China.
Thirty years old in 1926 Chiang Kai-shek came to power	In May, Chiang Kai-shek came to power as the chairman of the Central Standing Committee of Kuomintang. He initiated his "Plan to Straighten Party Affairs" and started to persecute the Communist Party. The struggle between the Chinese Communist Party and Kuomingtang intensified.
Beginning of the Northward Expedition	On July 9, the National Revolutionary Army started the War of Northward Expedition to eliminate the northern warlords and to unite the country.
Thirty one years old in 1927	On April 18, Chiang Kai-shek established the National Government in Nanjing. On August 9, the Communist Part organised the Autumn Harvest Uprising among the farmers living at the border area between Hunan and Jiangxi provinces.
Armed conflict between the Chinese Communist Party and Kuomingtang	In October, Mao Zedong set up the first Communist rural base at Jinggangshan area in Jiangxi. From there, various uprising broke out all over the country and military bases were established in a number of rural areas. In the meantime, the Kuomintang army started to round up the Communist Party army.

Thirty two years old in 1928 Two rubber factories under Aik Hoe company	The Tan brothers' rubber business had grown in scale while Aik Hoe became the biggest player in the rubber industry and owned two factories — one at Kim Chuan Road and the other at Xin Jian Guang.
The Ji'nan Massacre	In the same year, when the Kuomintang army were en-route on their Northward Expedition to take over Ji'nan City in Shandong Province, Japanese troops intercepted the Kuomintang army, occupied Ji'nan City and killed more than 6,000 Chinese soldiers and civilians. This incident was known historically as the Ji'nan Massacre. In Singapore, Tan Kah Kee started a fundraising committee in aid of the Ji'nan Massacre survivors. On December 29, Zhang Xueliang, a military and political strongman of the Chinese Northeast Army, submitted to the Kuomintang. The Northward Expedition of the Nanjing Government succeeded and China was unified.
Thirty three years old in 1929	On October 23, the New York stock market collapsed, sending the global economy into an unprecedentedly panic. Stock markets plummeted, factories and banks closed down, businesses went bankrupt, workers lost jobs, international trade dwindled, and the prices of raw products slumped. The economic crisis impacted almost everywhere in the world and persisted till 1933.

Thirty five years old in 1931 The September 18th Incident	On September 18, Japan expanded its invasion of China and sent troops to occupy the Three Eastern Provinces. This is historically known as the September 18 Incident (Mukden Incident), which led to Japan's full-scale invasion of China.
Thirty six years old in 1932	The rubber industry in Singapore and Malaya was also affected by the global economic crisis. Rubber demand on the international market dried up, plunging prices to 7 cents per pound, which was a far cry from the price of $1.80 straits dollars per pound in 1925. As a result, many rubber plantations stopped tapping, rubber factories closed down, rubber production reduced significantly, and rubber workers lost their jobs.
Big rubber businesses suffered	Big rubber businesses and owners of big rubber plantations made huge losses and they ran into financial difficulties. The rubber businesses of Lim Nee Soon and Tan Kah Kee were badly hit in the economic crisis. Tan Lark Sye's Aik Hoe and Lee Kong Chian's Lee Rubber, being new entrants to the rubber business with smaller scales and investments, did not suffer as much. Moreover, since the big rubber businesses and big plantations closed one after another, they had more room to maneouvre and grow.

Thirty seven years old in 1933 Sponsored Jimei	In the same year, Tan Kah Kee started to cut back on his business and leased his rubber factories to former subordinates. The rubber factory at Muar was leased to Tan Lark Sye's Aik Hoe company. However, it was agreed that part of the profits must be used to fund the Xiamen University and Jimei School. In the same year, Tan Lark Sye and Tan Boon Kue started to donate 500 straits dollars every month to Jimei School for its expenditures. On January 30, 1933, Hitler came to power in Germany, and established the Fascist Regime.
Forty years old in 1936 Donated 50,00 straits dollars to Xiamen University	In the same year, Tan Kah Kee raised 160,000 straits dollars to buy a 400-acres plot of rubber plantation and used the profit generated to fund the Xiamen University. Tan Lark Sye contributed 50,000 straits dollars in donation. In May, the Italian Fascists occupied Ethiopia. In July, Germany and Italian troops incurred into Spain.
The Xi'an Incident	On December 12, Zhang Xueliang initiated the Xi'an Incident and cornered Chiang Kai-shek into stopping his civil war and turning his efforts to fight against Japan.
Forty one years old in 1937 Chairman of the Rubber Trade Association	Starting from 1937, Tan Lark Sye served as the Chairman of the Rubber Trade Association of Singapore and later the Chairman of Rubber Processing Association, effectively becoming the leader of the rubber industry. The Rubber Trade Association of Singapore was founded in 1918.

	In the aftermath of the Ji'nan Massacre, Tan Kah Kee raised funds in aid of the victims. The Rubber Trade Association donated about 25% of the total amount of over 200,000 straits dollars.
	After Tan Lark Sye became chairman in 1937, he worked with Lee Kong Chian and various other leaders to develop and expand the Association's work. The Rubber Trade Association had more than 180 members by 1950. Tan Lark Sye and Lee Kong Chian each donated 200,000 straits dollars and bought the entire Windsor Building to be used as the Association's foundation property.
	In1933, the July 7 Incident broke out in China. In responce to Tan Kah Kee's call for aid, the Rubber Trade Association donated 1.29 million straits dollars to support the Anti-Japanese War.
The July 7th Incident	On July 7, the Japanese army attacked the Chinese army at Lugouqiao, near Beijing. The incident was known historically as the July 7th Lugouqiao Incident, which marked the beginning of a full-scale Sino–Japanese war.
	In August, Japan invaded Shanghai and met with strong resistance from the Chinese army. The city was lost to the invaders in November.
The Nanjing Massacre	In December, Japan attacked and occupied Nanjing, massacring more than 300,000 people. This was known historically as the Nanjing Massacre.

	In September, Kuomintang published the Announcement of Co-operation between the Kuomintang and the Communist Party to join forces against the Japanese army.
The Nanyang General Fundraising Committee	Tan Kah Kee organised the Singapore Fundraising Committee and collected 10 million straits dollars to support the Anti-Japanese War. The following year, he called on all communities in Southeast Asia to set up the Nanyang Overseas Chinese General Fundraising Committee in aid of the Refugees in China. Tan Kah Kee served as its chairman and Tan Lark Sye was elected as the representative of Singapore.
	In November, German, Japan and Italy formed the Fascist Axis.
Forty two years old in 1938 Expansion of Aik Hoe	After 13 years of growth, Tan Lark Sye's Aik Hoe Rubber Company had become the biggest rubber company in Singapore and Malaya. He broke through the stranglehold of foreign firms and sold his rubber directly to European and American buyers. He set up representative offices in New York and London to monitor the export of rubber.
	Aik Hoe also bought rubber plantations in Singapore and Malaya (it owned over 3,000 acres of rubber trees at Gelang Patah of Johor alone). His business spanned across all the rubber-producing Southeast Asian countries, covering the main commercial ports of Malaya, Indonesia, Thailand, and Vietnam.

Restructure Aik Hoe with More Investment	In October, Aik Hoe Rubber Company restructured into Aik Hoe (Private) Co. Ltd. With a registered and paid-up capital of 1 million straits dollars respectively, Aik Hoe became a big corporation.
Forty three years old in 1939 Donated to the Chinese Chamber of Commerce and Industry	In 1939, Tan Kah Kee rallied for a building for use by the Chinese Chamber of Commerce and Industry. Tan Lark Sye donated 50,000 straits dollars in the name of his brother Tan Boon Kue. The money covered 25% of the construction cost of the meeting hall and the library. In the same year, Tan Lark Sye bought 1 million straits dollars of public bonds and channeled the interests earned to fund Jimei School.
Forty three years old in 1939	From March to September 1, German and Italian armies attacked and occupied Czechoslovakia, Albania, and Poland.
Outbreak of the Second World War	On September 3, Great Britain and France declared war on Germany. The Second World War broke out.
Forty four years old in 1940	The registered capital of Aik Hoe was increased to 2 million straits dollars.
Forty five years old in 1941 Served as the vice-Chairman of the Singapore Chinese Chamber of Commerce and Industry	In March, Tan Lark Sye was elected the vice-Chairman of the Singapore Chinese Chamber of Commerce and Industry. During his term in office, he actively supported Tan Kah Kee's Nanyang Overseas Chinese Committee in sponsoring the Anti-Japanese War.

The Pacific War Japanese warplanes bombed Singapore	On December 7, 1941 Japan bombed Pearl Harbour in the United States' Territory of Hawaii. The Pacific War broke out. Japan then attacked and invaded the Philippines, Hong Kong, Malaya, Singapore, Indonesia, and Burma. On December 8, the Japanese army entered Kota Bahru in Northern Malaya, while sending bombers into Singapore.
Forty six years old in 1942 Sent money back to China	In January, before Singapore fell to Japan, Tan Kah Kee talked to Tan Lark Sye about contingency plans for the impending attack and urged Lark Sye to deposit money in China for future use. Taking his advice, Tan Lark Sye sent 70 million Chinese Yuan back to China with instruction that Jimei School could tap on the money when in need. Before Singapore was occupied by Japanese army, Tan Lark Sye took refuge on an outlying islet of Indonesia for half a year. His businesses were suspended. After he came back to Singapore, Tan Lark Sye was arrested and tortured by the Japanese army. On February 7, Japanese army entered Singapore via Jurong.
Singapore was occupied by Japanese	On February 15, British commander Arthur Percival surrendered to the Japanese army. Singapore fell into Japanese hands.

	For three years and eight months after the surrender, Japan carried out a bloody and terror-driven reign. Tens of thousands of Chinese in Singapore and Malaya were killed, while the local Chinese were forced to contribute 50 million straits dollars as "tributary money". Under the predation and enslavement of Japan, all businesses languished and the people lived in a horrendous state.
	Anti-Japanese activists of all races from Singapore and Malaya, together with the Malayan Communist Party, organised an armed resistance force. Taking advantage of the forests in Malaya, they fought a guerrilla warfare against Japanese. Later, Force 136, which was set up by Lim Bo Seng and British Captain John Davis, also participated in the Anti-Japanese battles.
Forty nine years old in 1945	On May 8, the Allied Forces attacked and captured Berlin. German surrendered unconditionally, ending the European War.
Atomic bombs dropped over Japan	On August 6 and 9, the United States dropped two atomic bombs respectively on Hiroshima and Nagasaki in Japan.
End of the Second World War	One September 2, Japan signed the Instrument of Surrender, thus ending the Second World War. Over 40 million soldiers and civilians die in the war, and military spending totalled at least US$1 trillion. Damages to property reached over US$1 trillion as well.

	The eight-year Anti-Japanese War had caused China the lives of 20 million soldiers and civilians, and more than US$150 billion in damaged properties and resources.
	In August 1945, Indonesia proclaimed independence and became a Republic.
Aik Hoe resumed business.	On September 5, the Tan brothers' Aik Hoe company resumed business. Eng Joo, the son of fourth brother Ko Dow, had returned with a master's degree in engineering from the United States and was put in an important position as the director cum manager of Aik Hoe. He eventually served as the Chairman of the Chinese Chamber of Commerce and Industry, the Chairman of the Rubber Trade Association, and the Chairman of the Rubber Industry Association.
Separating governance over Singapore and Malaya	In October, the British formed the Malayan Union of 9 Malayan states and the Straits Settlements of Penang and Malacca, with Singapore being excluded from the Union as a colony of England. From then on, Singapore and Malaya were governed separately.
Fifty years old in 1946 Controlled Rubber Trade	During the early post-war days, Britain set up military governments in Malaya and Singapore. Rubber became a controlled commodity and was monopolised by the British Government agencies. Rubber firms had to sell rubber to the purchasing agents from London at a fixed price of 36 cents per pound. Therefore, rubber firms were not able to sell rubber in free markets. Tan Lark Sye appealed many times for a free trade of rubber.

	In July, Kuomintang fell out with the Chinese Communist Party. A full-scale civil war erupted in China. On July 4, Philippines became independent from the United States. A cold war started between the United States and Soviet Union. Both groups tried hard to influence the world by ways of conspiracy in politics, economy and ideology.
Fifty one years old in 1947	On January 1, the British Government lifted the rubber trade control and free trade was resumed. The price of rubber increased gradually. Aik Hoe was able to grow in strength.
Two tycoons in rubber industry	In the following years into the 1950s, Tan Lark Sye's Aik Hoe and Lee Kong Chian's Lee Rubber were recognised as the two key players in the rubber industry of Southeast Asia. On August 14, India and Pakistan proclaimed independence from British governance.
Fifty two years old in 1948	From 1948 to 1952, Tan Lark Sye served as the chairman of Ee Hoe Hean Club.
Ee Hoe Hean Club	The first chairman of the club was Tan Kah Kee. The club was established in 1895 and was once the place for important social activities, including Tan Kah Kee's efforts to support the Anti-Japanese War in China. On February 1, the Malayans rose up to oppose the Malayan Union system, as they were not given more power of autonomy. England promptly changed the political entering from Malayan Union to Federation of Malaya. The Malayan states became autonomous regions under the central

	governance of the British Government. However, within the Federation, it was hard for people from India and China who were not born in Malaya to gain citizenship. As a result, Chinese immigrants strongly opposed the system. They went on strikes that at times turned violent, forcing businesses to close.
"State of Emergency"	In June, the British Government declared that Singapore and Malaya were in a "state of emergency" and the "Emergency Act" was hence enacted.
Fifty three years old in 1949	In February, Aik Hoe increased its paid-up capital from 1 million to 2 million straits dollars. The company was moved to 5-7 Beach Road.
	In the same year, the civil war between Kuomintang and the Communist Party in China was escalating, with Kuomintang suffering one defeat after another. On April 23, Nanjing was seized by the CPC. Chiang Kai-shek retreated southwardly and finally withdrew to Taiwan.
CPC in power	On October 1, Mao Zedong proclaimed the establishment of the People's Republic of China on the Tian'anmen in Beijing.
Fifty four years old in 1950

Chairman of the Singapore Chinese Chamber of Commerce and Industry | On March 6, Tan Lark Sye was elected Chairman of the Singapore Chinese Chamber of Commerce and Industry, which was founded in 1906 as the supreme body of Chinese businessmen in Singapore.

On March 15, when Tan Lark Sye first took office, he organised a fundraising event and donated 300,000 straits dollars to the building fund of the University of Malaya. |

Chairman of Hokkien Huay Kuan	In the same year, Tan Lark Sye was elected the chairman of the Singapore Hokkien Huay Kuan, succeeding Tan Kah Kee. He remained elected in the subsequent years, until just before he passed away.
	Also in this year, before Tan Kah Kee went back to live in China, he called in the directors and proclaimed Tan Lark Sye to be his successor, citing Tan Lark Sye's resolute perseverance in fighting for things that should have been done.
	In September, under the leadership of Tan Lark Sye, the Hokkien Huay Kuan collected 1.5 million straits dollars for its education fund.
	The Hokkien Huay Kuan was founded in 1860. It was the biggest clan association in Singapore, and had five affiliated schools. Tan Lark Sye was the Chairman of the Board of Directors of these schools. During his tenure, the Hokkien Huay Kuan built new school buildings for Chong Hock School, Kong Hwa School and Nan Chiau High School.
Outbreak of Korean War 1950 Rubber prices on the rise	On June 25, the Korean War between North Korea and South Korea broke out. The United States and China were dragged into the war on opposite sides until the war ended on July 27, 1953.
	Being a strategic material, rubber was bought up and stockpiled by European and American countries and members from the Soviet bloc. Due to the intense bidding, prices of rubber shot through the roof.

	In July, rubber prices went up from 95 cents per pound in June, before the Korean War to $1.20 in July.
	Prices rose again in August to hit $1.47, and it went on rising in subsequent months.
	The Korean War was a golden opportunity for the rubber industry in Singapore and Malaya. Tan Lark Sye's Aik Hoe reaped huge profits during this period.
Aik Hoe factory was razed	On July 27, Aik Hoe's big rubber factory at Kim Chuan Road was set on fire, apparently due to a labour dispute over wages.
	The sprawling factory employed 800 male workers and over 300 female workers. The fire burnt down most of the buildings, together with about 5,000 tons of rubber inventory. Damages amounted to about 10 million straits dollars. Fortunately, the factory was insured for a total of 7 million straits dollars from four insurance companies, thus mitigating the loss.
	After the fire, Aik Hoe set up temporary factories and continued producing rubber while the factory was being rebuilt. When news of the fire reached London, rubber prices there rose immediately. This indicated the impact of Aik Hoe in the rubber market.
Fifty five years old in 1951	In January, rubber prices hit 2.18 straits dollars per pound. Though it had suffered the devastating fire, Aik Hoe continued to grow from strength to strength by virtue of its solid foundation.

Control over foreign currencies	After the Second World War, the British Government imposed strict control over foreign exchange in Singapore and Malaya to forbid transfer of money outside the pound-sterling zone.
Organising fundraising activities	In the same year, Tan Lark Sye organised a fundraising event at the Singapore Chinese Chamber of Commerce and Industry, raising over 200,000 straits dollars for the Anti-Tuberculosis Association.
Fifty six years old in 1952	During his tenure in the Chamber, Tan Lark Sye pursued the issues of liberal use of languages in Legislatives Assembly and the rights of citizenship for the Chinese in Singapore. He also mobilised the public to participate in politics and stand for election in the Legislative Assembly.
Fight for citizenship	In February 1951, the Chinese Chamber of Commerce and Industry submitted a memorandum on behalf of the local Chinese to the British Government, appealing for a relaxing of policy on granting citizenship to non-British Chinese. Another memorandum was submitted in February 1952, which was rejected verbally by the Governor on October 20.
Removing restriction on languages	In 1954, the Chinese Chamber of Commerce and Industry proposed, through its representative at the Legislative Assembly, Tan Chin Tuan, that the Language Restriction Bill should be abolished. In January 1955, the Chamber mobilised all the local communities and the public to sign a petition that would be submitted to the Queen, asking for a multi-lingual system in the Legislative Assembly.

	After the Second World War, Tan Lark Sye had already adopted Singapore and Malaya as his home. In September 1950, he said, "Since the Second World War, I have come to realise that Malaya is doubtlessly my hometown." Therefore, he fought valiantly for citizenship and political right for the Chinese.
	On August 15, 1955, Viscount Alan Lennox-Boyd, the Secretary of State for the Colonies, visited Singapore. The Chinese Chamber and its affiliated commercial bodies organised a petition delegate of 1,600 people. They waited at the Kallang Airport, with slogans in hands, to appeal to the Secretary. In response, Lennox-Boyd maintained that the local government had the right to resolve the problem. On February 9, 1956, the Legislative Assembly passed the motion that English, Chinese, Malay and Tamil could be used as the languages for deliberation in the Parliament.
	The Civil Rights Bill was finally approved at the Legislative Assembly in July, 1957. Under the bill, residents who had lived in the country for 8 years could apply for citizenship. Registration for citizenship began in earnest on November 1, and the Chinese Chamber of Commerce and Industry helped the Government to register more than 200,000 people.
Fifty seven years old in 1953	After the Second World War, more Chinese schools were started every year. In 1950, there were 301 Chinese schools in Singapore, with total enrolment of 74,053 students and 1,949 teachers. In 1951, these were increased to 1,261 Chinese schools in Malaya, 221,050 students and 5,981 teachers.

Problems with higher education and teacher training options	Students of Chinese high schools wanting to enter a university after graduation, and supply of high school teachers were two major problems faced by Chinese schools. At that time, there was only one English-medium university in Singapore and Malaya, which was the University of Malaya. For political reasons, it was impossible for students to go to universities in China and the trained Chinese teachers could not come to teach in Singapore or Malaya. Therefore, there was a real need to set up a local Chinese university to fill up this vacuum.
Tan Lark Sye proposed to set up a university.	On January 16, 1954, Tan Lark Sye, then Chairman of the Hokkien Huay Kuan, gave a speech at the joint meeting of the executive committee. He suggested setting up a Chinese university and he pledged 5 million straits dollars on the spot. He called on the local communities to donate money to the cause, saying, "In order to preserve Chinese culture for posterity, I feel that it is necessary to set up a university. The present situation that students of our Chinese high schools not having a place to continue their studies has forced upon me the imperative decision to establish a university."
Support from all quarters	Tan Lark Sye's proposal was met with a resounding response from the commercial and industrial circles, the cultural and educational circles, and the labourers in the Chinese communities in Singapore and Malaya. However, the vice-chancellor of the University of Malaya, Sir Sydney Caine, and a few others thought it was not necessary to set up another university.

	Despite the opposition, well-known Chinese businessmen voiced their support for the proposal.
Opinions shared by well-known Chinese businessmen	Tan Siak Kew, then Chairman of the Singapore Chinese Chamber of Commerce and Industry, supported Tan Lark Sye's proposal. He believed that most of the Chinese living here had already adopted Singapore as their homeland, so establishing a Chinese university to nurture their children to serve the local community would indeed be a worthwhile endeavour.
	Ko Teck Kin, the vice Chairman of the Chinese Chamber of Commerce and Industry, said, "The establishment of a Chinese university will not only preserve and promote Chinese culture, but also improve the communication among various local cultures. …Mr. Tan is my old friend for many years, I know him as a person who would do what he said. With him as the champion, a university in Malaya will soon come true."
	Rubber tycoon Lee Kong Chian said, "Some people would be afraid that another university would cause dissension among the ethnic groups in Malaya. This is not true. The spirit of Chinese culture lies in the belief that 'all the people in the world are brothers'. We are trying every effort to promote harmony among the ethnic groups, and to help young people from different ethnic groups understand each other and to cooperate with each other."

	Lien Ying Chow, the Chairman of Overseas Union Bank, Ltd., said, "Mr. Tan Lark Sye is a resolute person with the financial capacity. His proposal to establish a Chinese university in Malaya is closely related to the effort to preserve Chinese culture. It will surely succeed."
	Aw Boon Haw, a prominent elderly tycoon in Singapore and Malaya, said, "I hope a Chinese university in Malaya will be established soon. This will not only be a blessing for the Chinese in Malaya, but also an effective bridge for academic communication between the east and the west. …The university should be an open university for students from all races, skin colours and religions."
Support from the Chinese Chamber	On January 21, a board meeting was held at the Chinese Chamber of Commerce and Industry. It was decided at the meeting that the Chamber supported Tan Lark Sye. At the same time, the meeting appointed the Chairman and the Vice Chairman of the Chamber to attend the annual conference of the Associated Chinese Chambers of Commerce and Industry of Malaya, which was held in Kuala Lumpur, and to present the proposal of establishing a Chinese Malayan university.
Land donation from Hokkien Huay Kuan	On January 23, Tan Lark Sye announced, in his capacity as the Chairman of Hokkien Huay Kuan, that the Hokkien Huay Kuan would donate 500 acres of land along Jurong Road to be the campus of the proposed university. He said, "From my point of view, the plot is located on high ground that is facing the sea and wide open space. This is an ideal place to set up the university."

Support from the Associated Chinese Chambers of Commerce and Industry of Malaya	On January 25, the Sixth Annual Conference of Associated Chinese Chambers of Commerce and Industry of Malaya passed the proposal unanimously and agreed to support the momentous plan of setting up a Chinese university.
Establishment of the University Preparatory Committee	On February 12, the directors of the Chinese Chamber of Commerce and Industry and 214 representatives from various Chinese communities convened for a meeting, at which Tan Lark Sye was elected as the Chairman of the committee. The meeting was held to discuss the plan of setting up a university. Tan Lark Sye and 12 other community associations were elected to form a Preparatory Committee (with 16 more luminaries of the community added to the list later).

Tan Lark Sye said at the meeting, "We will set up a university and it will be a success. ...You don't need to worry about the fund, for at least the first 10 years."

On February 18, Sir Malcolm MacDonald, British Commissioner-General to South East Asia, had two meetings with Tan Lark Sye and his associates. MacDonald suggested putting off the establishment of a new university until the expansion of University of Malaya was completed.

On February 19, Tunku Abdul Rahman, the Chairman of UMNO Malaya, said in a speech, "The local Malays do not oppose the establishment of a Chinese university." |

New university named Nanyang University	On February 20, the Preparatory Committee held its first meeting, at which the name of the new university was decided to be Nanyang University. The two characters "Nanyang" were used to commemorate the achievements of the forefathers when they first came south as pioneers of the land.
Declaration of the Establishment of Nanyang University	On April 7, the Preparatory Committee published a Declaration of the Establishment of Nanyang University. Four main reasons were listed, namely: (1) to open an avenue of further studies for high school graduates; (2) to train teachers for high schools; (3) to train talents with special skills for the region; and (4) to meet the demands of the growing population (6.7 million people in Singapore and Malaya combined).
Forming the Executive Committee	On May 19, the Preparatory Committee accomplished its tasks and the Singapore Committee of Nanyang University was officially set up. Among the members of the Preparatory Committee, 14 were elected into the Executive Committee. They were Tan Lark Sye, Aw Boon Haw, Tan Siak Kew, Ko Teck Kin, Yeo Chan Boon, Lien Ying Chow, George E. Lee, Lee Leung Ki, Foo Chee Fong, Kuah Chin Lai, and Ng Aik Huan. At the Executive Committee's first meeting on May 20, Tan Lark Sye was elected to be its Chairman.

	Tan Lark Sye announced at the meeting that he would donate 5 million straits dollars for the construction of Nanyang University. 2 million straits dollars would be paid upfront to set up the university and the rest will be paid over ten years after Nanyang University was set up.
	At the meeting, Lien Ying Chow also promised to donate 250,000 straits dollars.
	On July 26, as the chairman of the Executive Committee, Tan Lark Sye officiated at the groundbreaking ceremony of the Jurong campus.
Groundbreaking Ceremony of Nanyang University	In his address at the groundbreaking ceremony of Nanyang University, Tan Lark Sye said, "I am very excited to officiate at the groundbreaking ceremony today. I hereby sow the seeds of Chinese culture upon this wasteland. I foresee the Chinese culture will shine forth perpetually from here across Malaya."
	On August 5, representatives of the Nanyang University committees from the various states of Singapore and Malaya held its first general assembly in Singapore. Tan Lark Sye was elected to be the Chairman of the general assembly. He said, "Some say that since I advocated for the founding of Nantah, they will support me. As a matter of fact, Nantah is established by all the overseas Chinese in Malaya, and everyone plays an important part; in the same way, only when everyone plays their part will this project succeed."

	On December 13, Lien Ying Chow went to the United States to look for President for the Nanyang University.
Fifty eight years old in 1954	On January 29, the British Government in Singapore approved the establishment of Nanyang University and exempted donations to the university from taxes.
	On August 10, Lee Kong Chian announced that he would donate 10% of the total amount of donations that Nanyang University received over the next five years (1953–1957).
	On August 18, the Special Fundraising Committee of Nanyang University held its first meeting and set a goal of raising 20 million straits dollars by 1955.
World Youth Assembly	On August 22, the Second World Youth Assembly was held in Singapore. Tan Lark Sye threw an official banquet to welcome the 600 representatives from different countries to showcase Chinese culture and the objectives of the founding of Nanyang University.
	In his welcome speech, Lark Sye said, "There are more than 3 million Chinese in Singapore and Malaya, and over 10 million Chinese living over the Southeast Asian islands. Nanyang University will ensure and promote education in our mother tongues as well as preserve the great Chinese culture. Nanyang University will be politically neutral and welcomes students from all territories. Admission to Nanyang University will not be confined to Chinese people. As for the teaching media, it will not be only in the Chinese language either."

	Since Tan Lark Sye called for the establishment of Nanyang University in October, people from all walks of life — wealthy businessmen, unionised labourers, people from the literary and education circles, and members of the public — responded enthusiastically by donating and raising money for the university through various avenues. Within 15 months from August 1953, over 80 fund raising events were organised.
Fundraising drive by Trishaw Workers	The most touching donation came from 1,577 trishaw workers. On April 20, 1954, trishaw workers from the Trishaw Workers' Union organised an island-wide fundraising drive in Singapore. All proceeds from their hard labour would go towards the University fund. The event collected more than 20,000 straits dollars for Nanyang University. In addition, the annual fundraising basketball tournament organised by the Malayan Chinese Sports Promotion Association raised more than 230,000 straits dollars, and the 1953 cohort of Chinese high schools graduate raised over 60,000 straits dollars by staging a four-nights cultural concert. Other fundraising efforts included the stage performance by local arts group like the Ping She Peking Opera Society, fundraising drives by taxi drivers, lorry drivers and construction workers, salaries donated the Dance Hostess Association, hairdressing and barbers, sales, song concerts, paintings, exhibitions, as well as personal donations.

Lin Yutang Incident	On October 2, Lin Yutang arrived in Singapore to take office as the President of Nanyang University.
	On October 15, Lin Yutang held its first university management meeting in secret, in absence of the Executive Committee members.
	Only after repeated insistence by the Executive Committee did Lin Yutang finally submit all meeting minutes, the preparatory budgetary expenditures reading to the opening of the University and the mid-term development budget to Tan Lark Sye, the chairman of the Executive Committee in mid-February, 1955. However, the size of the budgets shocked everyone. For instance: staff remuneration between January and August 1955 was 320,000 straits dollars, and the salaries for the professors were higher than their counterparts in the United States. Added to this, lecturers would get 150,000 straits dollars of furniture subsidy and 240,000 straits dollars of travel subsidy (most travelling first class).
	Lin Yutang appointed his own son-in-law as the administrative secretary, his daughter Lin Taiyi the secretary in the University President's office, and his nephew Lin Guorong as the chief accountant. It smelled too strongly of nepotism, implicating the Lin's running their family university.

	In his budgets, Lin Yutang proposed to set up a University Funds Trustees' Committee. He requested the Executive Committee to turn over the 20 million straits dollars collected thus far to be placed under the discretions of the Committee, while the Executive Committee would have no rights to interfere. Lin's budget was disclosed to the public by the Executive Committee, and the society responded in an uproar. Despite repeated attempts by Tan Lark Sye and other members of the Nanyang University Committee to negotiate patiently with Lin Yutang, all the efforts ended in frustration. Lin Yutang even intended to appoint David Marshall as his lawyer to sue the committee for him, but Marshall declined.
300,000 straits dollars of Dismissal Package	On April 3, 1955, Lin Yutang and his cronies accepted a dismissal package worth 305,203 straits dollars and left the University. On April 7, the Nanyang University Committee held a meeting and set up a seven-member Recruitment Committee. At the meeting, Tan Lark Sye pledged to pay for the entire dismissal compensation in order that the University Fund would remain intact.
Recruitment Committee	The Recruitment Committee immediately started head hunting for the University President and faculty members. Several months later, the first batch of the teaching staff was announced with much contribution from Pan Guoqu (Pan Shou). Mr. Pan, at the opening of the university, was appointed

	Secretary General of Nanyang University. He was a calligraphist and a poet well known both at home and abroad being awarded the cultural medals by the Singapore and France governments. On November 20, Lim Lian Teng from Penang announced that he would donate 500,000 straits dollars to the University for the construction of the Library. On December 3, at the welcome party for Tan Lark Sye and fellow delegates to Penang, Low Kim Swi from Penang announced that he would donate 200,000 straits dollars to Nanyang University. Low Kim Swi and Tan Lark Sye were classmates in Jimei School and they used to help each other in their studies. Low was resolutely supportive of the establishment of Nanyang University, lobbying earnestly and successfully for Nanyang University in Malaya.
Fifty nine years old in 1955	On February 12, entrance examinations were held in Singapore and Malaya for pre-university classes. More than 400 students were enrolled. On June 15, pre-university classes started, with 420 students attending lessons in The Chinese High School and Chung Cheng High School. On December 12, the pre-university classes held their final examination.
Election under the Linde Constitution	In April, a legislative election under the Linde Constitution was held in Singapore. The results: 10 seats to the Labour Front, 4 seats to the Progressive Party, 3 seats to the People's Action Party, 3 seats to the UMNO-MCA alliance, and 2 seats to the Democratic Party.

	Labour Font formed a coalition government with the UMNO-MCA, with David Saul Marshall, the party leader of the Labour Front, becoming the Chief Minister.
	The People's Action Party was recently formed on November 21, 1954. Four candidates were fielded for the election and 3 won seats in the assembly (Lee Kuan Yew, Lim Chin Siong, Goh Chew Chuan), It was a respectable support rate.
	According to the Linde Constitution, the Legislative Assembly was then made up of 32 members: 25 seats were allocated to elected MPs, while 4 seats were reserved for nominated MPs and 3 seats for ex-officio ministers (Department of Justice, Department of Finance, and Department of Administration). The Governor served as the Chairman of the Assembly.
Sixty years old in 1956	On March 3, the results of the entrance examination for Nanyang University were released. The three colleges of Arts, Sciences, and Business enrolled a total of 330 students (excluding students enrolled through the pre-university classes).
	On March 5, the Management Committee — responsible administration of Nanyang University — was set up. Chang Tian Tze, the Dean of the College of Arts, was made the Chairman of the committee.

Opening of Nanyang University	On March 15, the Opening Ceremony of Nanyang University was held on her newly completed campus. The day everyone in Singapore and Malaya were looking forward to had finally arrived. The moment the University Flag was raised in front of the Library building, the thousand-strong crowd shouted "Long live, Nanyang University!" Tan Lark Sye, the Chairman of the Executive Committee, emotional in his opening address, saying, "Today is the most glorious day for overseas Chinese. Hundreds of years ago, we came south across the treacherous seas and suffered torments and hardship. Today, we have, by our own strength and endeavour, built our own university! Today, the University is finally opened!" Chief Minister David Marshall attended the ceremony and offered his congratulations on the opening of Nanyang University. Loke Wan Tho also announced his donation of 300,000 straits dollars for the construction of the College of Science.
573 new students	On March 24, Nanyang University welcomed her inaugural batch of 573 students, comprising 277 students for the College of Science, 256 students for the College of Arts, and 40 students for the College of Business. On March 30, the students started their classes. The day was scheduled the Founding Day of Nanyang University.

Pro-independence Assembly	On March 19, while the British Parliament Delegation visited Singapore, tens of thousands of pro-independence party members and members of the public assembled at the Kallang Airport, shouting slogans of independence and making passionate speeches.
Failure of the negotiation for independence	In April, a delegation consisting 13 representatives from Singapore's political parties, led by David Marshall, went to London to negotiate for the independence of Singapore while staying within the British Commonwealth. The appeal was rejected by the British Government. Marshall resigned from the position of Chief Minister after returning to Singapore. He was succeeded by his colleague Lim Yew Hock.
Hock Lee bus riots	Prior to this, anti-colonial government movements by democratic, leftist, labour and student organisation held demonstrations and strikes in Singapore. In April 1955, workers from the Hock Lee Amalgamated Bus Company went on strike to protest against the sacking of workers by the bus company. The police intervened while some students from Chinese high schools turned up to support the workers. On May 12, the police entered the bus depot and tried to disperse the strikers. This led to a riot causing 4 deaths and many injuries.
	In September 1956, the Government took actions. Unions and cultural societies deemed to be pro-communist were closed down, and political leaders, union leaders and student leaders were arrested. As a result, a riot broke out in October.

Sixty one years old in 1957 Rubber industry controlled by British Government	Britain had always dominated over the rubber industry of Singapore and Malaya. The rubber trading centres of the world were located in London and New York. Quality verification standards and trading terms were set by Britain and the union of western rubber firms. Tan Lark Sye and other local rubber traders always wanted to break through this stranglehold. In 1952, under the pressure from the western firms, the British Government published the Rubber Packaging and Distribution Act and set up the Rubber Export Registration Bureau to enforce the Act. Under the Act, British and American rubber companies could complain to the bureau on grading of rubber and demand indemnity. Once the complaint was verified to be true, the rubber manufacturers from Singapore and Malaya would be heavily penalised. 204 complaints were lodged in 1956 alone, which caused a great outcry among the rubber producers in Singapore and Malaya.
London rubber meeting	In May, a delegation of 5 representatives of Singapore's rubber producers (Tan Lark Sye, Tan Eng Joo, Ng Quee Lam, Soon Kwee Choon, Yan Puay Chui), led by Tan Lark Sye, the Chairman of the Rubber Trade Association, attended a meeting in London to resolve issues between British and Malayan rubber traders.

	Before they left for London, at the sending-off party at Tanjong Rhu Club (which Tan Lark Sye was the founder and chairman), Tan Lark Sye said passionately, "Today, the rubber packaging and export industry of Singapore and Malaya has come down with consumption (tuberculosis)… For over ten years while I served as the Chairman of the Rubber Trade Association, I had rivalled with the European and Western monopoly over rubber trade." "Now that the Rubber Export Registration Bureau is set up, we hear more of such cases. Now, prices were slashed by as much as 2–3 pence (per pound) each time we export our rubber… As a result, the rubber producers cannot make profits, and they are also losing their capitals. So, as I have ever mentioned before, we have all come down with consumption." "So, the aim of our trip is to see how they are going to suck our blood and by how much… However, we are going to do everything we can to find a 'new cure' for the disease."
Proposal of local delivery	At the London Meeting, Tan Lark Sye suggested that rubber could be delivered locally by Singapore rubber producers to the foreign buyers. He also appealed to the British buyers to set up offices in Singapore. In this way, the problems concerning quality and price cutting could be solved. The buyers could then verify the quality of the rubber before closing a deal.

	A party was given in Tanjong Rhu Club again to welcome Tan Lark Sye and his delegates home. Tan Lark Sye reported the achievements of the trip, which included impressing upon the British companies the importance of the Singapore Rubber Trade Association in the rubber industry of Singapore and Malaya, to have drawn attention from the opinions of the British companies to those of the Singapore Chinese rubber traders, and to have made clear the fact that the London trading companies were bloodsuckers.
Establishment of the Rubber Industry Association	After the delegation returned to Singapore, several negotiations were held between the Rubber Trade Association and the Western Rubber Traders Association. As a result, the Malayan Rubber Industry Association was founded, with Tan Lark Sye being elected as the founding Chairman. A joint statement was issued to proclaim that the birth of the Association would elevate the international status of the Singapore–Malayan rubber industry. This was a major breakthrough by Chinese rubber traders in fighting for their trading rights. Western companies and the European and American rubber industries started paying attention to the power of Chinese traders. In the same year, on an inspection visit to his company in Bangkok, Tan Lark Sye donated 500,000 baht to the Hokkien Association of Thailand to fund the development of local Chinese schools.

Internal Self-governance Agreement	In March of the same year, a delegation of representatives from Singapore's various political parties, led by Chief Minister Lim Yew Hock, went to London again to negotiate for the independence of Singapore. The British Government decided to only grant internal self-governance status to Singapore. An agreement was signed, which included the following main points:
	(1) Singapore would become an autonomous territory; (2) All 51 MPs of the legislative assembly would be universally elected; (3) The title of Chief Minister would be changed to "Prime Minister"; (4) The office and title of Governorship would be abolished, and a local would be appointed as the Yang di-Pertuan Negara; (5) Britain would retain control over defence and foreign affairs matters as well as the right to suspend the implementation of the Constitution; (6) An Internal Security Council, which would consist of three representatives each from Britain and Singapore and one from Malaya. Britain shall chair the Council.
Malaya gains independence	On August 31, Malaya gained independence from the colonial governance of Great Britain.
	As the degree's awarded by Nanyang University were not recognised by the Singapore Government and the academic standard of Nanyang University was in doubt, Nanyang University wrote to the Government on November 13 and agreed to invite international scholars to form a Commission of Enquiry to evaluate the academic standards of Nanyang University.

Sixty two years old in 1958	On March 9, the Nanyang University Act (Draft) was submitted to the legislative assembly (approved in March 1959).
Completion Ceremony of Nanyang University	On March 30, the Founding Day of Nanyang University, a Completion Ceremony was held to celebrate the completion of the campus building project. Over 100,000 spectators turned up in force, rendering the entire stretch of Jurong Road impassable to vehicles. A banner was strung across the frontage of the University Library Building, sporting an inspiring greeting to Nanyang University, which read "As the wind travels ten thousand miles, the great work (of the University) shall last for a thousand years (长风万里, 大业千秋)". In his speech, Tan Lark Sye said, "The most urgent task for Nanyang University at the moment is to uplift science and the scientific approach, while her mission is to facilitate the exploration of the various ethnic cultures and learning of multiple languages. In Southeast Asia, people who know English but not Chinese are walling themselves up in a progressively smaller world. More so in the world, not knowing Chinese is to deny oneself one half of the world." At that time, the Nanyang University campus, designed by the architect Ng Keng Siang presented a splendid landscape "beauty on every hills and affection on every branches" (树树尽相思).

Sixty three years old in 1959 Venturing into banking and insurance	1950s was the heyday of Tan Lark Sye's business empire. Apart from their core rubber business, the Tan brothers also diversified into banking and insurance business. Tan Lark Sye and his brother Tan Boon Kue served successively as the board Chairman of Asia Insurance Co. Ltd. and Asia Life Insurance Co. Ltd. Lark Sye also served as a director of Oversea-Chinese Banking Corp., the board Chairman of the Hong Kong Chiyu Bank, the board Chairman of Nanyang Siang Pau, and the Chairman of Singapore Tung Ann District Guild.
People's Action Party in power	In May, a general election of the legislative assembly was held in Singapore according to the Agreement of Self-governance. Several political parties participated in the election. People's Action Party fielded 51 candidates to contest in all the electoral districts and won 43 seats, thus earning the right to form the government. On June 3, the wholly-elected Government of Singapore was formed. Lee Kuan Yew, Secretary-General of PAP, became Prime Minister.
Donation from Hokkien Huay Kuan	On July 21, Hokkien Huay Kuan donated 600,000 straits dollars at the urging of its Chairman, Tan Lark Sye, for the construction of the Nanyang University Auditorium.
Two reports	On July 22, a five-member Commission of Enquiry, led by the Vice-chancellor of University of Western Australia, S. L. Prescott, compiled a damning report of Nanyang University, faulting her in many aspects.

	On July 23, Education Minister Yong Nyuk Lin assigned Dr. Gwee Ah Leng and others to set up another Review Committee of Nanyang University to evaluate Prescott's report and formulate the procedures and scope of restructuring Nanyang University. On November 20, the Gwee Ah Leng Committee published its own report that consisted of 18 suggestions to completely overhaul Nanyang University, which riled the Executive Committee.
Sixty four years old in 1960	On November 1, Dr. Chuang Chu Lin was appointed as Vice-President of Nanyang University to replace the duties of the Management Committee to look after the running of the university.
Recognition of degrees awarded to inaugural graduates	On February 8, Finance Minister Goh Keng Swee announced that the degrees awarded to the inaugural graduates of Nanyang University were recognised by the government. As for future graduates, the validation of Nanyang degrees would depend on the outcome of its restructuring and the improvement of its academic standards.
	On February 10, the Education Minister made a statement on the policy regarding Nanyang University at the legislative assembly, that the report by Gwee Ah Leng and his team was accepted in principle.

	On February 11, Low Geok Swee, Vice Chairman of the Penang Committee of Nanyang University, visited Singapore and met with Tan Lark Sye. He strongly opposed the proposal in the government statement that foreign students would account for only 15% of the new students intake of Nanyang University, as this stance would go against the original objectives of setting up the University.
First convocation	On April 2, the first convocation was held in Nanyang University, at which 437 students graduated. Most of them went on to work as teachers in the Chinese schools in Singapore and Malaya. Hence the immediate staffing shortage in Chinese high schools was resolved. Nanyang University was awash with festive joy on convocation day. Tan Lark Sye spoke at the convocation, "As the saying goes, 'Everything is difficult at the beginning.' Look at the founding histories of the universities in the world; how many universities had suffered so much obstacles and obstruction as Nanyang University? Yet how many of them could have started as stable as we did, and grew as fast as us? … We should be proud of ourselves for coming so far while we are still in the early years of the university."
Sixty five years old in 1960 Second convocation	On March 3, the second convocation ceremony was held in Nanyang University. 344 students graduated this year. In his speech, Education Minister Yong Nyuk Lin affirmed the performance of the first batch of graduates who were working in the various government bodies.

	Tan Lark Sye also gave a speech at the ceremony. He encouraged the students, "Before you leave the university, I have departing words for our graduates of Nanyang University — vow to contribute to the wellbeing of people; be loyal, brave and modest; be ever eager for academic and career achievements. You are the new blood of the society, the vanguard of the country. Apply your youthful vigour to work for the society and fortify our country."
Malaysia Plan	In May, Tungku Abdul Rahman, Chief Minister of the Federation of Malaya, disclosed his "Malaysia Plan" when he was attending a banquet for the foreign press in Singapore. He proposed to merge Malaya, Singapore, Sarawak, Sabah, and Brunei into one single country.
	The People's Action Party Government agreed to join Malaysia, while retaining autonomy in education and labour matters.
	In August, a rift appeared within the People's Action Party. Some MPs and party members left and formed the Barisan Socialis to oppose the Malaysia Plan.
	On September 1, 1962, a referendum was call to vote on the decision to join Malaysia. The result was a resounding "Yes".

Sixty six years old in 1962 Formation of the Nanyang University Council	On July 14, the First Nanyang University Council was formed in accordance with the Nanyang University Act published in 1959. Tan Lark Sye was elected as the Chairman. The Council had 19 members — one representative each from the 12 states in Singapore and Malaya, 3 nominated by the Singapore Government (less than that suggested by the government), 2 representatives each from the University Academic Affairs Committee and the University Alumni Society.
Sixty seven years old in 1963 "Operation Cold Store"	On February 2, the Internal Security Council of the Singapore Government carried out "Operation Cold Store", arresting leaders and activists from the allegedly pro-communist Barisan Socialis, unions, cultural and education organisations.
Establishment of Malaysia	On September 16, Malaysia was established as a single nation consisting of the Federation of Malaya, Singapore, Sarawak, and Sabah. Tungku Abdul Rahman took office as the first Prime Minister.
Singapore Election	In September, Singapore held its legislative assembly election. Barisan Socialis and other political parties also entered the election. Eventually, People's Action Party won the election again.
Lark Sye losses citizenship.	On September 22, Tan Lark Sye's citizenship was revoked.

Lark Sye quit as Chairman	On February 25, Tan Lark Sye tendered his resignation as Chairman of the Nanyang University Council. Low Geok Swee stepped in as interim Chairman.
	The Indonesia Government, led by the President Soekarno, strongly opposed the establishment of Malaysia. Therefore, it severed diplomatic relations with Malaysia. At the same time, Indonesia followed a confrontation policy and sent agents to plant bombs in Singapore and Malaya, killing and injuring many. The confrontation also caused huge economic loss from entrepôt trade in rubber, and other products with Indonesia.
Sixty eight years old in 1964 Agreement between government and Nanyang University	On June 5, an agreement between the Singapore Government and Nanyang University was signed. A joint statement was announced, which *inter alia* included the following main points: Once Nanyang University was restructured, the government would give Nanyang University the same treatment as the University of Singapore, and the degrees awarded by Nanyang University would be officially recognised.
	On June 27, the Nanyang University Student Union was disbanded by the Singapore Government.
	On July 1, Vice President of Nanyang University Dr. Chuang Chu Lin resigned.
	On July 8, Low Geok Swee, the acting chairman of the Nanyang University Council, quit from all his responsibilities in Nanyang University.

	On July 20, the Second Nanyang Council held its first meeting. Ko Teck Kin was elected as Chairman and Tan Chyi Guek as Vice Chairman. Henceforth, the Singapore Government would be directly involved in the decision making and administration of Nanyang University.
Changes within Nanyang University	Since quitting the position of Chairman of the Nanyang University Council, Tan Lark Sye had completely washed his hands off university affairs. Nanyang University went through a sea of change from 1965 to 1979, especially in her academic structure, courses, personnel, teaching medium, and student enrolment. Eventually, she became a university with English as the main teaching language. Finally, in 1980, Nanyang University merged with the University of Singapore to form the National University of Singapore.
Sixty nine years old in 1965 Relationship between Singapore and Malaysia	After the establishment of Malaysia, the Singapore Government had many differences in opinions from the ruling UMNO Party. With continuous instigations by the racists, two racial riots erupted in Singapore in July and September in 1964. Tungku Abdul Rahman, the Prime Minister of Malaysia, decided that Singapore had to leave Malaysia in order to avert disastrous consequences caused by the tense relationship between Singapore and Malaysia. In August, the Prime Minister of Singapore was informed of the decision.

Independence of Singapore	On August 9, the Malaysia and Singapore governments announced simultaneously that Singapore had separated from Malaysia to become an independent country. In December, Singapore legislative assembly approved an Amendment to the Constitution. Singapore became a republic.
Seventy years old in 1966 Cutting back operations of rubber business	1950s was the heyday for Tan Lark Sye's rubber business. During the 1960s, artificial rubber gained wider use (half of the world rubber consumption in 1960 were artificial rubber). In addition, Indonesia enforced an embargo on Singapore because of the confrontation policy. Aik Hoe Group was forced to diversify its business into other areas.
Investing in industrial sector	Since the early 1960s, Tan Lark Sye started to diversify capital into industries such as Tasek Cement Ltd., Malaya Paper Mill, and the United Pulp & Paper Company Ltd. In addition, Aik Hoe also invested in hospitality and construction industries. Tan Lark Sye served as the Board Chairman of Ipoh Cement Co. Ltd., which was the largest cement producer in Malaysia whose products were sold in Singapore and Malaysia as well as other regional markets.
Tan Boon Kue passed away	In the same year, Tan Boon Kue, the third brother who had started and developed the family businesses together with Tan Lark Sye, passed away. The two brothers were the decision makers of Aik Hoe. They were very close, and worked well together, with Boon Kue taking care of the rubber plantations, rubber factories and the insurance industry while Lark Sye focusing on rubber trading.

	Boon Kue served as the Chairman of Aik Hoe and Asia Insurance Co. Ltd. He was also the Chairman of the Tung Ann District Guild and the Po Chiak Keng Temple Tan Clan Ancestral Altar, and a director of United Overseas Bank.
	Tan Boon Kue left behind six sons: Yung Siong, Yung Chuan, Yung Wan, Yung Hing, Yung Yam, and Yung Khiam, and six daughters.
Seventy two years old in 1968 Building an empire from scratch	Tan Lark Sye and his brothers came south with empty hands. Through sheer hard work and perseverance, they built and grew their businesses, and finally became tycoons. After the war, the second generation of the Tan family joined the management team. Since them, Aik Hoe Group integrated ownership and management in the hands of the family. The Tan family had over 200 family members in Singapore and Malaysia.
	Aik Hoe Group subsidiaries included: Aik Hoe, Hiap Hoe, Chip Hoe, Hua Ek, Ee Chang, Tan Eng Joo Engineering, Union Construction, Asia Insurance, Asia Life Insurance, Tasek Cement Co. Ltd., Malaya Paper Mill, and the United Pulp & Paper Company Ltd.
	The Tan brothers helped each other. The shares and directorship of Aik Hoe were evenly distributed among the brothers, and their siblings.
Wives and children	Tan Lark Sye had 4 sons by his first wife Cheong Kim Nan: Eng Wah, Eng Yi, Eng Keong, Eng Bo; he had another 5 sons by his second wife Chua Siew Ching: Eng Shun, Eng Seng, Eng Han, Eng Sin, Eng Sen. In addition, they had three daughters; Shu Zhen, Lan Ying, and Xiu Ying.

Seventy four years old in 1970 Lark Sye's view on money	Tan Lark Sye's perception of money determined the approach of his social behaviour in community in his lifetime. He once said that for charity "giving money is very much like defecating." At a fundraising event for Nanyang University, he addressed the wealthy businessmen, "It may not be beneficial, even harmful, to the children if a rich man leaves his fortune to his offsprings." Therefore he was always generous with his donations for education. He also gave financial assistance to many friends and business associates. On September 9, in a speech at the Hokkien Huay Kuan's school building fundraising event, Lark Sye said, "Most people thought that hoarding wealth, properties to benefit their descendants is a way to enrich them. However, this is not the case today. For example, the former Chairman of the Hokkien Huay Kuan Mr. Tan Kah Kee spent all his wealth on promoting education, grooming thousands of talented youths so that they can contribute to the nation. His act of generosity benefitted not just his own children but others' children as well. In this, Mr. Tan set up a fine example of true patriotism and nationalism for us. Some rich men may have a mountain of fortune, yet are stingy towards giving to the society. What good would that lead to?"

Lark Sye's way of life	Tan Lark Sye was very much influenced by the altruism of Tan Kah Kee. He established Nanyang University, led the Chinese Chamber of Commerce and Industry to fight for citizenship, fought for the liberation of the rubber business in Singapore and Malaya, donated generously towards the Anti-Japanese War, education and charity. He always kept his promises. He was magnanimous, fearless and resolute. Tan Kah Kee never counted his gains or losses when he expended his wealth to promote education for the sake of his hometown, his country and his people. The personalities and mannerism of these two great men were so alike that they are a reflection of each other.
Seventy six years old in 1972 Tan Lark Sye Passed Away	On September 11, Tan Lark Sye died of a heart attack. People all over Singapore and Malaysia felt the loss keenly and organised a grand memorial service and funeral for him. With the flag of Nanyang University draped over his coffin, Tan Lark Sye's funeral was attended by thousands of people. They prayed that his spirit and the spirit of Nanyang University would live forever.
Bronze Sculpture	On September 14, Nanyang University Council decided to cast a bronze sculpture of Tan Lark Sye in memory of his merits. The sculpture would be erected in Nanyang University campus, to be honoured and respected by posterity.

	A ceremony was held on June 15, 1974, for the erection of the bronze sculpture. The family of the late Tan Lark Sye pledged to donate $500,000 to the university to set up the "Tan Lark Sye Scholarship".
	Singapore Hokkien Huay Kuan decided in February 1982 to cast a sculpture each for Tan Lark Sye, Tan Kah Kee and Lee Kong Chian in memory of their contributions.
Memory Forever	It has been 25 years since Tan Lark Sye passed away, but Nanyang University, all her students, the lakes, hills, trees, buildings and hostels on the campus are still in remembrance of this great man.

An elegiac couplet from Hokkien Huay Kuan.

A pair of elegiac couplet from the Tan Lark Sye Funeral Committee.

A pair of epitaph couplet at Tan Lark Sye's tomb (1).

A pair of epitaph couplet at Tan Lark Sye's tomb (3).

Chapter 9

Collection of Mr. Tan Lark Sye's Important Speeches

9.1 Call for the Establishment of Nanyang University

Tan Lark Sye, Chairman of Hokkien Huay Kuan, proposed to set up a Chinese university at the joint meeting of executive and supervisory committees of the Hokkien Huay Kuan on January 16, 1953, and announced that he would donate $5 million towards the project. The proposal was met with enthusiastic response. The following is the speech Tan Lark Sye made at the meeting.

We should not allow the Chinese culture to be eradicated in Malaya; instead, we should defend and promote it. Why? There are currently tens of thousands of Chinese students in the schools, a large number of whom would graduate each year. Some time ago, they could return to mainland China for their higher education, but that door is closed to them now. Our children are forced into believing that the future of their career and higher education lies only with English education. Although there have been some talk that the University of Malaya will set up a Chinese Department, it still remains only rolling thunder without rainfall with the excuse that they could not find suitable staff. However, their Malay Department will be set up soon. Since the setting up of a Chinese Department in the University of Malaya remains remote, we need to set up a Chinese university to defend and promote our Chinese culture.

Furthermore, the prevailing political situation will deny our Chinese high school graduates an opportunity of higher education. We have no choice but to set up a Chinese university ourselves. I mentioned this idea two years ago. I pointed out then that the university should be set up within three years or latest within five years; otherwise, Chinese culture would start to decline in Malaya.

This time around Hokkien Huay Kuan decided to continue campaigning for the education foundation fund in two ways. First, Ai Tong and Chongfu schools will be rebuilt at an estimated cost of $1 million for which Hokkien Huay Kuan will campaign for the funds. This amount will form a comfortable pool for our five schools. Towards this project I hereby pledge to donate $200,000. Second, if the public responds positively towards our campaign for building of the university, we will probably raise between three to five million dollars. In the event, I will personally donate the same amount. My fellow members of the Huay Kuan, if you agree with me on the needs of setting up a university, rise to the challenge and set a good example towards making this dream come true. If we can reach this target in our funding campaign, I will mobilise and coordinate with the various parties in and around this region to join hands in this monumental work of seeing this university for the Chinese to come to being at an early date.

Setting up this university may cost hundreds of millions and even more, if we expect this university to be comparable with those established institutions in Britain and United States. Therefore, we will start by setting up a few colleges and gradually expand our university. In this way, our young people will be able to receive primary, secondary and tertiary education, and our culture will be preserved for the future.

Two years ago, I was ready to propose setting up a Chinese university. My plan, however, was thwarted when my rubber factory was burned to the ground by arsonists; otherwise it would have been put into motion two years ago. Today, I present this proposal again, not because I am wealthy now, but because our Chinese community felt strongly that this university must be established. I will, therefore, devote all my wealth in cooperation with my fellow Chinese compatriots in our joint endeavour.

9.2 Declaration of the Establishment of Nanyang University

The Nanyang University Preparatory Committee issued "the Declaration of the Establishment of Nanyang University" on April 7, 1953 with Tan Lark Sye in his capacity as Chairman of the committee. This declaration unveiled four reasons for establishing Nanyang University and its two distinguishing characteristics.

For a long time, the Chinese in Malaya wanted to establish a University. The plan was incubated some two years ago, as our grand vision of future needs. Unfortunately, it did not materialise as the timing was not right. On January 16, 1953, Mr. Tan Lark Sye put forward the proposal again. This time his call was answered enthusiastically by people from all walks of life. Local Chinese readily came forward to donate land and money. In our assessment of the needs now and beyond, we have concluded that the establishment of a Chinese university cannot be further delayed for the following reasons:

First, to set up an avenue for high school graduates to further their studies. As the Chinese saying goes, it takes ten years to grow a tree but a hundred year to groom a person. The grooming process is not done when students finish their secondary education; they need to go for further studies before their potentials can be fully realised. There are over 300,000 students in the Chinese schools today, and five to six hundreds of them graduate from high school every year. This figure is set to increase with each coming year. However, the current situation has deprived our children of the chances for higher education. In the past they could go to universities on mainland China, but the current political climate has ruled that option out. As for the University of Malaya here, the entrance requirement placed much emphasis on English, not to mention the limited places available. It could not even admit all the graduates from English schools and had to reject a large number of them. I have seen bright young people stuck in this higher education dilemma. Our education has come to naught and the local community loses all these potential talents. This is such a sad situation!

Second, to groom teachers for secondary schools. The high schools in South-east Asia have traditionally depended on mainland China for recruitment of teachers. However, given the political situation, this source of recruitment has dried up. Meanwhile, the number of teachers we have now is dwindling either due to retirement or leaving this country for various reasons. With the growing number of Chinese schools over the years, the shortage of secondary school teachers is becoming increasingly serious. If we do not act now, the development of education would be subject to the pressure of dwindling teacher population and eventually leading to closing down of schools.

Third, to nurture people with specialised knowledge and skills for our country. With the impending independence of our country, there is a great need for people with talents to be deployed in the many nation building projects. Yet, if you look around our society today, how many people have received university education? How many people possess specialised skills? If we do not build up a pool of talents, we will be panicky when the needs arise. How then can we claim self-reliance and autonomy, or even independence! The primary purpose of university education is to groom talents. Even small Western countries have more than one university. The University of Malaya was established in October 1949 and current enrolment is only 850 students, and this number is totally inadequate to meet our country. That is why we can no longer afford to delay our decision to establish a university to foster our talented people who will steer our nation towards independence and beyond.

Fourth, to meet the needs of a growing population. The entire Malaya Federation has a population of 6.7 million. It is not excessive to set up three more universities in terms of educational development standards in modern countries. With only 8.5 million people, Australia already has seven universities, each of which has its own track record. In this perspective, Malaya is behind time with its one and only university.

Putting all these four points together, establishing a university has become our pressing agenda. At the moment, we have decided to set up four colleges of arts, science, business and technology, which together shall be known as the "Nanyang University". The curricula are organised with reference to that of internationally renowned universities, by overseas recruited scholars. All young people entering this University shall be treated alike, regardless of their ethnic background, in the noble spirit of democracy and education, which, we believe, will be good news for all the people in this country.

Given its historical background and special circumstances of its birth, Nanyang University will possess two distinctive characteristics besides the common objectives of its becoming an internationally renowned university:

First, as the bridge between the ancient Eastern culture, which is profound in breadth and depth, and the brilliant Western culture, which is deeply rooted and widely influential. Together, they form the main framework of world culture. Singapore is situated at the pivotal point of the confluence of these two cultures. For this reason, an important agenda of universities in Singapore should be to serve as a conduit for both cultural systems to mingle and prosper. This is where Nanyang University can complement the University of Malaya. While the University of Malaya emphasises English, Nanyang University would place equal emphasis on Chinese, English and Malay to meet the practical demands for academic research, so that scholars may be well grounded in the local languages without fear of falling behind international level. In this way, Nanyang University can function as the bridge linking both Chinese and Western cultures.

Second, as a centre for developing the Malayan culture. Malaya is a land where the Chinese, Malays and Indians live in harmony while having frequent social and cultural interactions. A distinctive feature of Nanyang University will be the study of these ethnic cultures and the amalgamation of their essences into a Malayan culture that shall have its pride of place in history. For this reason, Nanyang University will focus its research efforts in subjects such as the geography, history, economy and language of the various ethnic groups in Malaya.

It has been two months since the idea of Nanyang University was mooted. The sheer amount of support and enthusiasm from the various quarters of society is a sign of how far our society has progressed. The Nanyang University Preparatory Committee was formed on February 11, 1953 in Singapore. Branches of the Preparatory Committee have been successively set up all over Malaya with overwhelming support. Preparations are now underway in earnest, and we will not stop until the University is born. My colleagues and I will spare no efforts to realise this university as a blessing to our country. We will not be distracted in our efforts and will remain true and sincere to our task. With this declaration, we place ourselves under the guidance of the government, society and leaders of all ethnic groups in this society!

9.3 Sowing the Seeds of Culture in this Wilderness

At the ground-breaking ceremony of the Nanyang University campus on July 26, 1953, Tan Lark Sye, Chairman of the Nanyang University Executive Committee, conveyed his wishes that the Chinese culture would "be as bright as the Sun and the Moon, and everlasting as the universe".

My fellow countrymen, today we hold the ground-breaking ceremony for Nanyang University. I am very excited here to preside over this ceremony. We have sowed the seeds of culture here, and our Chinese culture will take root in Malaya, shining like the Sun and the Moon, and everlasting as the universe. The flames of Chinese culture shall never be extinguished. Our culture in Malaya will live on forever, just as Malaya shall live on forever. Last year, out of my worries about the future of our culture, I could not help coming forward to campaign for the establishment of Nanyang University. Our aim was to ensure that the Chinese culture could last forever here in this country. Today, you see an untamed wilderness all around you here, but it is here that the Chinese culture will take root and thrive forever.

Malaya is a haven where the English, Chinese, Malays, and Indians coexist. The Chinese need to preserve their own identity and culture. Otherwise, we will become a people without identity. In thirty years' time or so, the local population will increase dramatically, and the Chinese population will increase by sixty to seventy percent. That is when we will need to be even more rooted in our cultural identity. It is for this reason that we are fighting hard today to preserve our culture for posterity.

Britain shows its political wisdom to grant independence to Malaya. However, if our Chinese culture do not take root and thrive, we would not be able to assist in preserving the independence of this country. Nanyang University will not only preserve Chinese culture, but also nurture talents to meet the future needs of Malaya. Many Britons have shown sympathy to the cause of Nanyang University, so it cannot be understood why there are undesirable elements among the Chinese here who are out to oppose and even sabotage the setting up of Nanyang University. Sabotaging the University would surely be akin to desecrating their own ancestors.

While I have made donations for the establishment of Nanyang University, I hope that all the Chinese people in Singapore and Malaya will share this load with me for the sake of our descendants. Nanyang University is not set up by me alone, but by all the Chinese people here. Do not give up your responsibility. When you come back here next year, this wilderness you see today will have been dramatically transformed by then. When Nanyang University campus is completed, this land shall become a cradle of talents. In order to meet the needs of a rising population in thirty years' time, not only will our university be expanded by then, there will be branch campuses in other parts of Malaya. With the Chinese community solidly behind us, Nanyang University will surely have a bright future!

9.4 The Status of the Chinese People Before and After the Japanese Occupation

Tan Lark Sye, Chairman of the Nanyang University Executive Committee, threw a banquet at the Tanjung Rhu Club on February 28, 1954 in honour of the famous female writer Dr. Han Suyin, who later became a volunteer campus doctor in Nanyang University. The following is Tan Lark Sye's speech that night.

It is my honour to welcome Mdm. Han Suyin here tonight. For the years since I settled down in Singapore, I have never read in newspaper anything as touching as the speech Mdm. Han gave at the joint press conference on February 15. She did not speak on political issues, but about the people. Some of the facts mentioned in her speech were things very few knew about. Even if they knew, they would not dare speak out, nor do they had the appropriate platform to do so even if they dared. For those among the tens of millions of Chinese in Southeast Asia who can read Chinese and have read what she has said, I am sure they would have been deeply moved.

It is a pity that those who cannot read Chinese would have no chance at all to read her speech. Even if they know about it, they would not feel as much for what she said as we felt. We are deeply impressed by her speech. The Chinese in Southeast would be well-regarded if we were as bold and outspoken as Mdm. Han. The fact is, the Chinese are scorned across Southeast Asia, even held in contempt in the West.

I still remember the days when Singapore was threatened by Japanese invasion. With a population of a million under the air raid and artillery bombing from the enemy, the Chinese did their best to maintain order and formed our own self-defense forces that took part in the Red Cross activities amid air raids. At the invitation of the Government, the Chinese Chamber of Commerce and Industry called on the Chinese to cooperate with the government and mobilised more than ten thousand people every day to help evacuate citizens, rescue the injured and construct defence facilities while dodging dozens of sorties daily by the enemy warplanes. When the Japanese army entered Kedah and Penang, the Governor of Singapore called upon the Chinese to rise up against the Japanese invaders. I attended a number of such meetings with the Governor. Back then, the Government heaped praises on the Chinese for our contributions. The Governor promised the leaders of the Chinese that should Singapore fall, he had made provisions for safe evacuation of the people. With this assurance, the Chinese contributed our efforts and resources generously. When the Japans pushed deeper into central Malaya, the Chinese requested the Government to arm them for armed resistance. Unfortunately, the Government did not truly want to arm the Chinese, until when the Japanese troops occupied Pontian, Johor, the Government then issued the Chinese five hundred old firearms, which were useless against the invading army. Inadequately armed, the Chinese resistance forces charged bravely into the battle front but little did we know on that the very next day, the British army blew up the Causeway. With no way of retreating, the Chinese resistance forces pressed on to Pontian and Batu Pahat to harass the enemy line, inflicting losses to the enemy. As a result of our resistance, the enemy hated the local Chinese. When they occupied Singapore, they conducted an unprecedented scale of census to massacre Chinese. The wiser ones among us had the premonition that by doing so, the Japanese Government wound cause great harm to the local Chinese after they took over the city.

In the first year of the Japanese occupation, they regarded Chinese as their enemies. Only after they failed to secure the support of the other ethnic groups did they seek our cooperation. The sea around Singapore and Malaya by then was full of the Allies' submarines that threatened the Japanese safety of vessels. In the end, the Japanese asked the Chinese to help transport food to ensure continuous supply for the five million people in Singapore and Malaya. Even when the Japanese surrendered, the Allies' battleships were anchored off Singapore waters for several days, pending landing while waiting for fresh command. As we all know, Malaya is a land where people of different ethnic groups live together. When the Japanese were vanquished with the British army sitting tight off-shore, Malaya was in a state of anarchy. If this situation was not handled properly, it could lead to many nasty incidents. However, as the Chinese had always striven to live peacefully with the other ethnic groups, the dreaded mass chaos never happened. There were a few incidences, but were amicably resolved through the mediation of local Chinese leaders.

During the Japanese occupation, although the price of rice was almost 100 dollars in "banana money" (Japanese occupation currency) per *kati* in the black market, the rationed rice provided by the Japanese troops cost only 10 cents in "banana money". After the British troops landed, the price of rice rocketed to 20 cents "straits dollar" per *kati*, which was a thousand-fold increase compared to the now-worthless "banana money". Tens of thousand of tons of rice left behind by the Japanese army were expropriated by the British Government, and it was inconceivable how much profit the British had reaped. Furthermore, the tens of thousand of tons of rubber left behind by the Japanese, which were looted from our local people, were also expropriated by the British Government when they took control of Singapore. During the period of over three years of Japanese occupation, their food, clothes and lodging were all looted from the local people. After the British retook Singapore, all these looted resources and properties that rightfully belonged to the local Chinese were labelled by the British as 'enemy property' and used as compensation for war losses. Those given priority to claim war loss compensation were mostly foreign businesses, leaving very little to benefit the local Chinese.

The Singapore government recently released new regulations on Chinese education, aimed at restricting Chinese education. The National Education Act adopted by the Federation of Malaya in 1952 stipulated that English and Malay were the official languages, and that all commercial book-keeping must be kept in English or Malay. Ostentatiously, this Act was put in place to enforce national education. However, by piling on more taxes and implementing the Business Registration Act, what the Government did amounted to eliminating the Chinese culture using the money collected from the local Chinese. While the Singaporean government might have announced in the education paper to increase subsidies to the Chinese schools, the amount granted was meagre and fraught with various restrictions. Since most of the local students were already citizens, therefore the Government was supposed to assume the responsibility of offering education to all citizens by way of subsidies. On the contrary, there was a consensus that the increment of this Government's subsidy to Chinese schools was miserly, negligible with the mounting taxation.

The Chinese have always lived in peace with the other ethnic groups here. We do not have excessive demands. What we want is just and equal treatment. Why have we been reduced to "lamb to the slaughter?" I hope that through her constant interaction with the Chinese here, Mdm. Han will have a clearer picture of our predicaments and inform the world of the plight the Malayan Chinese are facing.

9.5 Hosting Delegates to the World Youth Congress

Tan Lark Sye, Chairman of the Nanyang University Executive Committee, held a banquet on August 22, 1954, for the hundreds of delegates attending the 2nd World Youth Congress in Singapore. The following is the speech delivered by Tan Lark Sye, in which he publicised the Chinese culture and reiterated the purpose of setting up Nanyang University.

Delegates to the World Youth Congress, honourable guests,

Tonight, on behalf of the members of Nanyang University, I have the honour of hosting a simple dinner here at the City Hall to welcome you to the World Youth Congress. With us tonight are key local government officials and leaders of all ethnic groups in Singapore. I am deeply honoured by your presence.

Nanyang University is going to be set up in Singapore. This is a higher educational institution urgently called for by the three million Chinese people in Singapore and Malaya. The Chinese community in Singapore and Malaya have voiced their unanimous support for the setting up of the University. Tonight's banquet can be perceived as a warm welcome and gratitude extended by all the three million Chinese people of Singapore and Malaya to you.

The delegates have travelled afar to see for themselves a young, beautiful and prosperous Singapore, which in many ways resemble your youthful spirit. I'd like to take this opportunity to say that, the prosperity of Singapore and Malaya today has been the result of joint effort of Chinese, Malays, Indians and English people through their sheer hard work for generations. For the Chinese community, their ancestors have been here in Nanyang archipelagos not less than a thousand years ago. In particular, during the last ten decades, the construction and prosperity of the local community has largely been due to active participation of the Chinese people. As a fellow Chinese, I am not here to glorify the contributions of the Chinese people, but to present the facts simply. Wherever they are, the Chinese people are peace-loving, caring for the place they live in and coexisting harmoniously with the other ethnic groups. This is part of our tradition and our nature. We do not have other excessive demands except for equitable treatment.

The Chinese culture has a history of over five thousand years. Countries, apart from China, that speak or use Chinese language and characters in their way of life include 750 million people in Japan, Korea and Annam (Vietnam). That is a proof that this language in term of its wide coverage is as venerable as the Sun and the Moon, and as permanent as the Sky and the Earth. In this context the three million Chinese people in Singapore and Malaya, and the ten million Chinese people in the Nanyang archipelagos need Nanyang University to preserve and develop their mother tongue, to safeguard our glorious Chinese culture, as well as to groom specialised talents for the societies and to contribute to world peace by way of spreading the Chinese culture of peace to all over the world.

Every year, there are about 400,000 students enrolled in the Chinese primary and secondary schools of Singapore and the Federation of Malaya, and there are about 1,000 high school graduates each year. This number is still growing relentlessly. To meet the demands posed by this situation, and to guarantee an avenue for these young people to continue their studies, it became imperative to establish Nanyang University as soon as possible.

Nanyang University will not be politically tainted. It will open its door to students from any region. Our students are not limited to the Chinese, and the teaching medium is not constrained to the Chinese language. We are grateful for the understanding, sympathy and assistance from the governments of Singapore and the Federation of Malaya, and for the spiritual and material support from people of all ethnic backgrounds. With all these support, Nanyang University can be established in a short period of time to meet the needs of the local community. Nanyang University is burdened with a great mission in which it will position itself as a melting pot for the integration of cultures of the various ethnic groups in Singapore and Malaya into a brilliant new culture leading to a fresh new chapter in human history.

Dear delegates, the agendas that have brought you here for this congress can be generalised under the category of cultural issues. In the next few days, you will deliberate over ideas to arrive at differing conclusions that are beneficial to humanity and the world. On behalf of Nanyang University, I propose a toast: to your generous guidance, unrelenting support and everlasting friendship with Nanyang University. Nanyang University will also promise its best towards an excellent education for our young people, who will follow in your illustrious footsteps. I hereby wish the Congress success and to all of you, happiness and health.

9.6 Call on the Public to Elect Their Assemblymen

The Chinese Chamber of Commerce and Industry held a rally in the Tanjong Pagar constituency on January 15, 1955, to call on the electorate to vote for their assemblymen to represent them in the coming Rendel Constitution election in April. The following is the speech delivered by Tan Lark Sye at the rally.

This coming April, Singapore is going to put a new constitution into effect: over 280,000 voters in the 25 electorates in Singapore will elect 25 assemblymen into the new legislative assembly, out of which the ruling party in the assembly will get to run six departments within the government. This is the British government's gesture to grant autonomy to Singapore by handing the governance of this country to its people, as well as the beginning of returning self-governance to the people and eventually allowing Singapore and Malaya to become independent. Even though the heads of the military, foreign affairs, finance and police departments are still appointed by the British government, the governance of commerce and industry, education, housing, transportation, healthcare, civil aviation, agriculture and social benefits will be handled by these elected assemblymen. In other words, Singapore has been granted autonomy over all internal affairs but not foreign affairs. Singapore is a state in which the Chinese, British, Malays and Indians live together, and jointly manage our government peacefully. The elected assemblymen will have the decisive power to formulate new or review old legislations as well as to vote on any proposals. Therefore, this general election that will signal our first step towards autonomy is of utmost importance to our people's welfare.

We know that the four ethnic groups living together here have already regarded this place as their homeland. However, Singapore's limited territory and growing population will pose challenges to our livelihood in the future. We need to come up with reasonable solutions to meet these challenges. This is what the legislative assembly is for, and that is why the election of assemblymen is so important to us. In view of this, the Chinese Chamber of Commerce and Industry has formed an Election Mobilisation Committee to call on all the people in the 25 electorates to work together; awaken their political awareness and appeal to the voters to actively participate in politics by exercising their entitled political right to cast their votes, so that truly competent people who are familiar with local affairs could be elected into the assembly to serve the people.

After the War, the British government had treated general elections in Singapore only as a formality, so only a few were elected to the Assembly. The Assembly was still under the control of the British government. The people know this very well from the past and this explains the general apathy of people towards politics. As a result the few elected assemblymen have been irrelevant to address the real issues and inspiration of the people. This year, the 280,000 voters in the 25 electorates of Singapore will be going to the polls. We should take an active interest in voting for the 25 assemblymen who can truly represent the people and take charge of the major affairs of Singapore. I believe that though Singapore is small and populous, it sits at a strategic confluence of the maritime routes between Europe, Asia, the Philippines, and Australia. It is also a natural harbour. If the country is well-governed, businesses, industries and economy in Singapore will flourish, and the people would be guaranteed a stable, happy and prosperous life.

How we can realise the prosperity of the Singaporean businesses and economy and improve our people's lives, hinges on the electorate districts working closely with the Chamber of Commerce to elect assemblymen who are truly concerned about the people. Singapore is like a headquarter and the neighbouring countries are like our manufactories. This headquarter may be small, but if we demonstrate good planning capabilities, that will put us in an advantageous position. Let me illustrate this point with some examples of the measures taken after the War.

Firstly, the government has yet to completely revoke food rationing since the War was over. While Singapore is not a rice-producing country, our neighbouring countries, such as Annam (Vietnam),

Siam (Thailand), and Burma (Myanmar) are known as the rice-bowls of the world. The farmers in these countries earn a meagre three to five straits dollars per *dan* (fifty kilograms) of rice for their toil, yet rice used to cost more than 100 dollars per *dan* in Singapore. Even now, it still costs dozens of dollars per *dan,* and the people have no access to cheap rice. This is one of the evils brought about by poor governance and stifling policies.

Secondly, since the War, businesses and industries have been severely constrained as a result of the government's foreign exchange policy. Without this stranglehold, Singapore could then capitalise on its strategic location at the confluence of maritime routes between Europe, Asia, the Philippines and Australia. Free trade with all the countries in the world and free flow of merchandises will attract capital investments from all over the world to develop our businesses and set up more factories here, which will contribute to universal employment. Instead, many of our people are unemployed and living in poverty. All these are the detrimental effects of the foreign exchange policy. We should look into this major problem seriously.

Thirdly is the housing problem in Singapore. Although the government has built houses in the eight or nine years after the War, there is still a severe shortage of housing, which is also a consequence of bad governance. The rent control policy and the prohibitive property tax have impeded the growth of the private housing developments. The government's attempts to build houses have failed to solve the severe shortage of housing. The government also intended to clear the slums, but after clearance of slums, they were replaced with houses with sky-high rentals which were beyond the reach of average people. Consequently, the land which used to house the poor is now inhabited by the rich, while the poor from the slums were deprived of their shabby shelters. The housing crunch and slums issue must be resolved through practical and fundamental solutions.

Fourthly is the issue of unequal education opportunities. Indians, British, Malays and Chinese are invariably paying taxes, but opportunities of education enjoyed by them have been variably inequitable. Such an undemocratic politics is a result of ungrateful assemblymen who have been oblivious of their own ethnicity and their ethnic culture.

Finally, the prosperity of Singapore and its businesses must be built on a sound industrial development, for only then can we ensure employment for everyone and a stable life. With a stable society comes growth in businesses and industries, and the economy will prosper. All these issues can be solved only at the legislative assembly.

Therefore, I sincerely appeal to everyone here tonight to take the election of assemblymen seriously and to participate actively in the election this April.

9.7 A Painstaking Report on the Lin Yutang Incident

The Nanyang University Executive Committee held its sixth meeting on March 25, 1955, at which Tan Lark Sye reported on the Lin Yutang Incident.

I am going to report what happened after our fifth meeting on February 17. Around four o'clock in the afternoon of the 18th, the lawyer David Marshall and Mr. Lim Yew Hock came to my office with the news that the Chancellor of the University, Mr. Lin Yutang, had appointed Mr. Marshall as his lawyer. However, Mr. Marshall said that he was sympathetic with Nanyang University, and wished that Nanyang University would succeed soon. He would hate to see anything untoward happen to this university. I told him then that matters were not that serious. We talked for a long time, and Mr. Marshall eventually suggested that the chancellor and I should talk to each other. I agreed immediately, for every time the chancellor invited me for a talk in the past, I had always shown up and never missed an appointment. Mr. Marshall then proceeded to call Mr. Lin and made an appointment for us to meet at the Cathay Building at five o'clock in the afternoon of the 19th. On the morning of the 19th, I read a statement by Mr. Lin from the press that he was going to negotiate a settlement with me, but the agenda that he elaborated in his press statement deviated from the intention of the prearranged talk. I was taken aback, but I made it to the appointment. However I had to invite Ko Teck Kin, Lien Ying Chow, Ng Aik Huan and Lim Keng Lian to come along to the meeting. After we arrived at the venue, the Chancellor also arrived, together with his son-in-law, and Hu Boyuan, Li Dongfang, Yan Wenyu and Yang Jiemei. Mr. Marshall invited me to speak first. I recounted the talk I had with Mr. Marshall in the afternoon of the 18th, and pointed out that I was invited to have a talk with the Chancellor, with no specific agenda. Then Mr. Marshall asked the Chancellor to speak. With a cool expression, Chancellor Lin targeted at me in his allegation, "You

166

can maneuver, I can anticipate." After a short pause, he continued, "I know you are the Chairman of Nanyang Siang Pau, and you were behind the news report yesterday." Lim Keng Lian interrupted, "That is not true. I am also a director of the newspaper and I know what had happened. Although Tan Lark Sye is the Chairman of the newspaper, neither he nor the members of the board come to the office unless there is an important meeting. Usually they do not interfere with affairs of the newspaper." The Chancellor proceeded to accuse me of breaking my promise, and elaborated my flaws and errors which put me in a bad light. After his lengthy speech, the Chancellor produced a note for me to sign, which was tantamount to me agreeing to the terms listed by him. I did not read it, nor did I dare to, for I did not know the details of his terms. I told him that I had no capacity to commit on behalf of Nanyang University, and that if he had any personal agenda, he should submit them to the university committee in writing. I would then convene a meeting to discuss his terms. Once they are approved by the committee, I would not contest them. The atmosphere at the so-called "negotiation" was very tense, with clear division taken by respective parties. Halfway through the "negotiation", they remained in the hall, while the committee members and I were led to another dining hall, with Mr. Marshall acting as the messenger for the two parties. However I reiterated that Nanyang University belongs to the public, so I had no capacity to negotiate with anyone on the University issue, especially with the Chancellor taking such a vicious stance. Needless to say, I felt I was humiliated. Apart from the humiliation and torture suffered in the hands of the Japanese soldiers during the Shonan period, I had never been so humiliated with slander slapped on my face on that day. I controlled my emotions and put up with it for the sake of the University. To avoid further confrontations, I left before the meeting ended. As the Chairman of Nanyang University, I have to look after the interests of the University and put these differences aside, including my humiliation, so as to resolve this issue amicably. The Chancellor made another statement in newspapers on February 20. For the sake of the University, I remained silent throughout even though I felt degraded by the Chancellor statement. All of you here can attest that I did not make any comments to the newspaper. When pressed by journalists, I kept saying that since the matter was being looked into by a special subcommittee, I could not interfere with their task. As soon as the subcommittee had reached a conclusion, I would report it to the general assembly of the University. As for the reports in the English newspapers regarding my handling of the University matters, I have never taken them seriously as there were gaps in making myself fully understood by the English press. All the issues on Nanyang University have been based on reports published on the Chinese newspapers. I'd like to take this opportunity to stress that the purpose of my campaigning to setup Nanyang University and the strong support from the Chinese community in Singapore and Malaya is to provide an opportunity for our young people to pursue their studies. It is purely out of my own conviction that I have willingly donated several millions of dollars. I have stated repeatedly that Nanyang University is a sacred academic institution that should be free from any political manipulation. No one in the University, from the Chancellor to the wardens should ever be involved in any political activities. It is because of our unambiguous conviction that we have earned the support from all sectors. Should I take on myself, then, for all these unforeseen troubles that have arisen today?

As for the Chancellor disclosing unilaterally all the correspondences between him and me, I have not verified them one by one, so I am not sure whether all have been published or some could be withheld any. The press have reported on Mr. Lien Ying Chow's trip to the United States to meet with Chancellor Lin, as well as the Chancellor's subsequent letter from the United States. Most of my letters to the Chancellor were sent after Mr. Lien returned to Singapore. These letters were written by people assigned by Mr. Lien or Mr. Ng Aik Huan and were free from my personal opinion. They were all vetted by the University Executive Committee, and Mr. Lien often revised them. I felt that these letters need not always be so formal, but Mr. Lien always took these correspondences as ordinary letters which were not regarded as contracts. My enthusiastic flattery in the appointment of the Chancellor was a matter of routine, in the context that all matters concerning Nanyang University are a public undertaking. Mr. Lien has always said so, and after deliberation, I subscribe to his view. I would do the same thing when I am engaging a manager to run my business. I would always be positive, not only to entrust the business to him but also to grant him year-end bonuses. However, when the manager keeps making wrong decisions that bring about losses every passing day since he came, how can I still grant him full authority and bonuses? I declare again that all the letters sent to the Chancellor were not of my sole initiative, and on all occasions more than half of the 11 Executive Committee members would have vetted them. Furthermore, even though I am the University founder, I have repeatedly reminded myself that I would not take credit for myself. By donating money and devoting myself to this university, I am only playing my part as a fellow Chinese passionate to serve our ethnic cause. Nanyang University is not my personal business. The current incident with the Chancellor came out of the blue. The uninformed may tend to believe that it is the result of personal grudges I bore towards the Chancellor. All matters of Nanyang University are always a public concern and they cannot be dealt with by me alone.

Members of the Committee, the successful establishment of Nanyang University has been completely attributed to the communal support of the people in Singapore, Malaya and Borneo. For now, it seems that everything is going well with the University, but upon scrutiny, it may not always be so. Ultimately, Nanyang University will be established against all odds, with all your wisdom. If you have any question to raise, I will try my best to enlighten you.

According to the minutes of the University meetings forwarded to me by the Chancellor, it has been decided that the monthly remuneration scale for professors is $1,500 to $2,000, while that of associate professors is between $1,200 to $1,700 dollars, $900 to $1,400 for lecturers, $600 to $850 for tutors, and $300 to $750 for teaching assistants. Their yearly increments are pegged at $50 per month up to 10 years. As such, the salary ceilings should be $2,340 for professors, $2,000 for associate professors, $1,600 for lecturers, $1,260 for tutors, and $900 for teaching assistants. I felt very worried after I read it, because I am afraid that Nanyang University may not be able to afford it. Our University relies on solicited donations, not on receivables. In that sense, the University is begging for handouts. We may be able to afford to run the University if it is run the same way as universities are run in China; but if the University is run the same way as the University of Malaya, we definitely cannot afford it.

9.8 The Proudest Day for the Overseas Chinese

Nanyang University finally started its classes on March 15, 1956. Tan Lark Sye, Chairman of the Executive Committee, officiated at the opening ceremony. In his speech, he said that it was the proudest day for all overseas Chinese.

I am here to declare loudly that today is the proudest day for overseas Chinese. Several hundred years ago, some Chinese people migrated here. Through hardships and tribulations, they have finally built a university with their own effort and hard work. This University starts its classes today.

In the past the government of our motherland, such as the Qing dynasty, failed to protect the rights and interests of overseas Chinese; instead, they turned a deaf ear to all slanders heaped on us by foreigners, and held the discriminations against us. However, the force of overseas Chinese was not demoralised. On the contrary, we contributed to the overthrow of the Qing dynasty. Today, whether Malaya will win independence or not depends on how we perceived this problem.

For dozens of years the overseas Chinese enjoyed no protection from their motherland, but inspite of this handicap, they still have built primary schools, secondary schools and even a university — Nanyang University, which starts its classes today. Therefore, I'd say that today is the proudest day for overseas Chinese.

We know that a sound established nation can only be built on its good citizens, and upbringing of good citizens depends on education. For this reason, Nanyang University is established in order to groom competent and good citizens for our country.

As the political power is still in the hands of others, the overseas Chinese pay the same taxes but receive unequal social benefits, especially in the field of education. Therefore, we should rely on ourselves for renewal.

Nanyang University is the first university for overseas Chinese. Hitherto Chinese secondary schools in Singapore and Malaya did not adopt a unified syllabus. Last year when Nanyang University offered prep courses, it was intended to adjust this discrepancy and bring about the various standards of secondary school turnouts to a common level which can satisfy the admission standards of the University. When the prep course came to an end, the students achieved excellent scores due to their hard work and strict discipline. I feel very relieved that they can meet the University admission requirements.

Now that Nanyang University has started its classes and the deans and professors engaged by us have all subscribed to the objectives and calls as per the Nanyang University Declaration. For long-term education goals, I hope that all registered students observe the school regulations and the instructions of the deans and the professors, and they should be doing well in their academic endeavour. I hope that all of the first batch of Nanyang University graduates will enjoy good premiums in politics and commerce after leaving the University and made valuable contributions to the society and make Nanyang University internationally known.

9.9 Autonomy, Independence and Citizenship for the Chinese

The newly elected and out-going presidents and vice presidents jointly threw a banquet for members of the management board of the Chinese Chamber of Commerce and Industry at the Tanjong Rhu Club. The following speech was delivered by Tan Lark Sye at the banquet on April 17, 1956.

The Chinese Chamber of Commerce is generally acknowledged by the local Chinese community as its supreme institution. Tonight, the four out-going and newly elected presidents and vice-presidents of the Chamber jointly hold a banquet for the new and out-going members of the board.

On this occasion, I would like to raise the issue of autonomy and independence of Singapore and Malaya in discussion with all of you present. Recently, Chief Minister David Marshall led a delegation to Britain to gain autonomy and independence for Singapore. In my opinion, given a number of outstanding domestic issues, the prospect for granting citizenship to us local Chinese may not be as hopeful even after eventual independence.

When the Colonial Secretary visited Singapore last year, he said that the citizenship issue could be resolved locally. The Secretary's statement should be taken as the British government's stance, but the local authorities had not put forward the issue of Chinese citizenship to the legislative assembly. There is no telling how this issue would be settled after our independence eventually. Someone recently raised a preposterous proposal that all those who were foreign born should be regarded as foreign residents and not be eligible for citizenship. We should be alerted to this preposterous proposal.

During the Second World War, Churchill and Roosevelt stated in the Atlantic Charter that all the affected nations should be given the right to decide their own future after the war. Great changes around us have picked up pace recently. The Federation of Malaya would become an independent state in August next year with the blessing of the British government. However our delegates were already in Britain negotiating for our own independence; but there were still outstanding issues in our domestic affairs that had not been resolved yet. The outcome would be that after our eventual independence, someone could claim that the Chinese people were foreign residents and did not have the right of universal suffrage.

In fact, the Chinese people being local residents here should never be afraid to fight for our citizenship. Otherwise, we would fail ourselves. This being a direct concern for the rights and interests of every Chinese here, we should endeavour to fight for it. As the supreme institution for the Chinese community, the Chinese Chamber of Commerce should spearhead this campaign. In case we would perish as martyr in this fight, it would be far better than to be regarded infamous by our posterity. Otherwise, if we should be expelled from this country in the future, it would be due to our passive response today.

I therefore strongly urge all Chinese to heighten their political awareness, and hope that the Chinese Chamber of Commerce would assume leadership in the endeavour for citizenship for the Chinese.

9.10 A Letter to the Education Minister to Straighten Out the Issue of Academic Degrees Conferred by Nanyang University

Tan Lark Sye, president of Executive Committee of Nanyang University, wrote to Chew Swee Kee, Education Minister of the Labour Front government, on May 4, 1956 to argue against the view that "Nanyang University has no right to confer academic degrees".

Dear Minister Swee Kee, I was alerted yesterday by a journalist from a Chinese paper on your view in The Strait Times that "Nanyang University has no right to confer academic degrees", to which I was asked to respond. At first, I could not believe it, but later I resigned myself to the situation. Initially, I could not believe because such comments would not have been made by a Minister of Education of an elected government. Furthermore, as a Chinese, you would not have made that comment as you would understand the great difficulties faced by the Chinese education here. The reason why I chose to believe because with an Education Minister such as yourself, and with some members of the Chinese community sharing your view, it was no wonder that you readily parted with this remarks. However after a close scrutiny of your comment, I could sum up your intentions in the following two points:

First, you intended to make students of Nanyang University feel that their future was hopeless, and thereby lose faith in the University.

Second, you intended to debase the reputation of Nanyang University such that it would lose the support of civic minded people in the community.

So, was it not true that you were trying to kill two birds with one stone by undermining the faith of our students and cutting off our support from the community? The Minister should question himself whether that was the way he discharge his ministerial function!

Nevertheless, I would like to respond candidly to your allegation:

First, Nanyang University has prevailed against all odds. The greater the setbacks, the harder we will fight on. Our objective is pure and beyond reproach; our faith in its setup is firm since it has now come into being, it will move on. As a Chinese, the Minister should be aware of the aspiration of the Chinese community. Commerce and manufactories may rise or fall, but education, which will benefit all people and bring about welfare for the community, will always flourish.

Second, Nanyang University is a public undertaking by the joint efforts of the three million Chinese people and other ethnic groups in Singapore and Malaya, apart from paying taxes to governments, who have also given beyond their means in money and in deeds to establish this University; to groom talents for the local community, and share the burden of education with the Government. They give rather than take, and pursue the cause for the common good rather than for profits. How is it that a government official, who is expected to encourage and facilitate such good causes, but on the contrary be so quick to obstruct and destroy it. Is this your way to prove your loyalty to your job in the implementation of your government policies as well as for the local community? Please enlighten me.

Third, classes at Nanyang University just started four weeks ago, for only one batch of freshmen. They were like one month old babies in a sense. What the University is now concerned is how our students progress in their pursuit of studies, how our academic staff conduct their lectures and courses, how our facilities be brought up-to-date, and whether our University can be characterised as an institution by practical mind and intellectual elegance? We are further concerned whether our graduates can contribute to the society by way of their intrinsic strength, performance and making meaningful statements. If they graduate from our University none the wiser and are of no contribution to the society, the University would be unworthy of its name, even if our academic degrees are recognised all over the world. If, however, our graduates can contribute to the society via their intrinsic strength, performance and meaningful utterance they will bring honour to Nanyang University, notwithstanding our academic degrees not being recognised. Moreover, it is still too early to judge whether our academic degrees will be recognised or not. Would it not be unwise of anyone to pass judgement prematurely?

Fourth, Nanyang University is in the legal process of seeking a status that it deserves. We would be eternally grateful if the Minister could help us along. Would the Minister be prepared to give us assistance?

Fifth, each university has its characteristics, style, priorities, and strengths, which differ from one university to another. Each university has its own value and purpose for its existence. If the one needs to shore up A to match B, would it not suffice to have B alone, rather than to have another A? It has become a matter of rules for universities to cooperate with and improve on each other. Is the Minister aware that the Science Faculties of Nanyang University and University of Malaya have started to jointly work on organising academic lectures? It is only now that I came to hear from you that one university should be led by another. This is something unprecedented.

Sixth, the relationship between Nanyang University and the Ministry of Education depends on that which already exists between the University of Malaya and the Ministry. Any move to impose something on Nanyang University that is different from that applied to the University of Malaya would be perceived as discrimination against Nanyang University, something that cannot be covered up.

Seventh, the education profile, moral judgement and evaluation ability of ministers of an elected government are subject to assessment by the electorate. Those who are competent and who can readily understand the passions of voters can always be elected again even if they are unsuccessful in their incumbent term. However those who are incompetent and who go against the passion of their electorate could not keep their position long, and when they leave, they go down in infamy. The opinions of a minister are not always representative of the public opinion. How can we nominate a government that implements policies against the wishes of the public? Would the people not call for a re-election and replace the government with a new one? As the Chinese saying goes, water can keep a boat afloat, it can capsize the boat just as well.

Before I end my letter, I have a personal note that I need to express. Please do bear with me and hear me out.

In three to five years' time, the graduates of Nanyang University will be able to serve the needs of Singapore, Malaya and Southeast Asia, and they will achieve greater heights than those graduates from other universities.

Best Regards.

9.11 Salvage Chinese Education and Culture

The following is the preface by Tan Lark Sye to the book *How Nanyang University Came Into Being*, published by Nanyang Culture Press in September 1956. The preface exposes the colonial government's intention to discriminate against and put a check on Chinese education, and reiterates the objectives of establishing Nanyang University.

At the time when WWII was still raging with victory of the Allied Forces still faraway in sight, American President Roosevelt and British Prime Minister Churchill unexpectedly made a joint declaration of the Atlantic Charter, which stated clearly that after the war colonialism would be abolished; autonomy and independence would be granted to all colonies, where its people would make their own decisions on religion and education, and no country should interfere in the internal affairs of another country. The Charter expressed particularly that ethnic culture and mother tongues should be respected. The brilliance of this Charter convinced the world that the Allies fought against invasion of freedom and democracy, for emancipating people of the colonies, and for helping the weaker nations. The spirits of this Charter served to provide a turning point in the warfare between the Allied Forces and the Axis with the former finally prevailing over the latter.

In 1945, Japan surrendered. Singapore and Malaya was liberated, and the British army returned. However, out of their scheme to establish a long-term foothold in this region for strategic or empire ambitions, the British recanted the Atlantic Charter. They separated Singapore from Malaya by assigning a new governor on each side of the straits, in a bid to isolate both territories. They then expanded the number of English schools vigorously and discriminated against mother tongue education, particularly against Chinese education. In 1947, various reports on the education in Singapore — like the

Barnes Report, blue paper reports and white paper reports etc. by the government, were commissioned one after another. Any recommendation that could suppress Chinese education were readily adopted by the Legislative Assembly. In 1951, the Business Act of the Federation of Malaya even went so far as to stipulate that all book-keeping should be kept in English. Step by step, the colonial government sought to create an environment in which Chinese would be rendered irrelevant and forced to die out. Hitherto of all the eight to nine hundred thousand students currently enrolled in schools across the whole of Malaya every year, half of them were from Chinese schools, with the rest of the students spreading out in English, Malay or Hindi schools. Most of the teachers in Chinese schools were from China, and graduates of Chinese high schools could freely choose to go to China to pursue their higher education. Today, it has become increasingly difficult for teachers from China to come here to teach, and the students who wish to pursue higher education in China are allowed to go but could not be allowed to return. Although the Singapore government has set up the University of Malaya, its enrolment was limited. Even students from English schools found it hard to get admitted, not to mention those from Chinese schools. Under this circumstance, the Chinese people in Singapore and Malaya are worried and lost, not knowing what the future will hold for us!

Over the 5,000 years of Chinese history, the Chinese language has been used as the tool for communication. It is used by no less than 750 million people in China, Korea, Japan and Vietnam. This is the best evidence to justify its existence. How, then, can one deny its value? Yet, today, shall three million plus Chinese in Singapore and Malaya stand aside to allow Chinese education and culture to die out in this new-born nation which we ourselves endeavoured to build and which we call our home? Can we stand to see our children and their posterity to live in oblivion of their ancestors and ethnic heritage!

It pains me every time I think of this precarious situation. So I came up with the idea of setting up a university modelled after that in China, as an effort to turn the tide and with the hope that the Chinese culture will continue to shine forever over Singapore,

Malaya and even the whole Southeast Asia. I harboured this idea for some time. When some close friends came by, I shared this idea with them and they also shared my concerns. However, drawing on the experience of universities around the world, including the University of Malaya here at home, we were reminded of the herculean task of raising a huge fund needed to build an university, as well as annual expenditures on running the university. Even if we could raise the requisite funds, would the government give consent to the proposed University? There was no certainty. Therefore I pondered over this for some time.

Considering the pressing urgency of the matter, I thought the time was ripe for me to bring up this issue at the general meeting of the Hokkien Huay Kuan on January 16, 1953. My suggestion to set up a Chinese university here was instantly greeted with thunderous applause. My reason was that this issue had a direct bearing on the future of Chinese culture in Singapore, Malaya and even Southeast Asia, and all the Chinese in this region should get involved in the project. In a few days, Chinese people all over Singapore and Malaya responded to my call in unison. Local Chinese newspapers such as the Nanyang Siang Pau and Sin Chew Jit Poh enthusiastically published commentaries in support of the campaign. Other Chinese language newspapers outside the region also followed suit. Nanyang Siang Pau even pioneered a generous donation with a statement to promote the cause. In February, a meeting was convened at the Singapore Chinese Chamber of Commerce and Industry, where a total of 278 representatives of various social groups turned up. The mood was fervent, and the delegates cheered the effort, chanting "Only Success, Not Failure". A preparatory committee for the university was formed, and the university was named "Nanyang University". However, at the same time, dissenting voices were heard from other quarters. Malcom MacDonald, High Commissioner of Britain in Southeast Asia, and Sir Sydney Caine, vice-chancellor of the University of Malaya, unexpectedly called me for a meeting. It was the first of a series that ensued. I went for all the meetings, together with Tan Siak Kew, president of the Singapore Chinese Chamber of Commerce, Ko Teck Kin, Lee Kong Chian, Lien Ying

Chow, Ng Aik Huan, and Tan Cheng Lock. Each of the meetings, which usually entailed heated exchanges, lasted several hours. They boil down to this: the government believed that since there was already a University of Malaya, why was it necessary to start another university? I refuted their option, saying "What we are going to build is a Chinese-style university that is very different from the University of Malaya, which only uses English as the teaching medium. The University of Malaya does not even have vacancies for all the applicants from English high schools. What chances do the students from Chinese high schools stand to have amid this mass of English school students clamouring for a place?" The meetings ended in a deadlock. Seeing how unyielding they are, we decided not to waste our breath any more. We stepped up efforts to prepare for the construction of the university. Fortunately, the various Nanyang University executive committees all over the region stood solidly behind the Preparatory Committee to provide all available resources and efforts into our project. We were not upset by obstruction, and picked ourselves up quickly when faced with set-backs. We were forced to register Nanyang University as a limited liability entity to circumvent the obstacles placed to frustrate our efforts. In May, when the registration was approved, Quah Chin Lai was elected to organise the development of the university campus. Thus, through two years of hard work, the five hundred acres of land donated by Hokkien Huay Kuan was dotted with row upon row of splendid-looking school buildings.

I am just a businessman who has been overseas for a long time. I may not be the wealthiest man in Singapore and Malaya, and I may be over ambitious in my call for building a university. It would be like attempting to raise a towering mountain with just one basket of soil. However, my boldness is founded on the strength of three million Chinese people, and I derive my guts from the determination of these three million Chinese people. Without the perseverance of the committee members and the unwavering support of all the Chinese people, Nanyang University would have become abortive halfway!

There is ancient saying, "To impart your son with a skill is a better gift than wealth." In the future society, it will be hard for one to earn a living without a specialised skill; what more will he need to build a successful career? I often use the metaphor of tide water to illustrate one's attitude towards wealth: when the tide comes in, we should harness it to irrigate the fields, and then the field would produce good yield. If we do nothing, we yield nothing too, and this swell of wealth is meaningless to us. Within moments, the tide will recede, as will our wealth. Therefore, if you know that your children are good learners, would you not want to contribute to nurture their talents. If you are wealthy and understand that money comes and goes like the tide, would you not want to put it to good use before it is too late.

Community work requires all who are concerned to give of their best according to their ability. There are always some onlookers who find excuses to pass the bucks. There are those who will contribute no matter what. Those who can afford are welcomed to contribute more, and those who have little resources need not be shy about contributing what little they can. If we just collect the underbelly hair of a thousand foxes, we can make a fur coat out of it; and the feathers of ten thousand birds can block a river so that one can cross it!

Nanyang Culture Press is compiling a book on how Nanyang University came into being. They approached me to say a few words for its publication. I was initially filled with mixed feelings, which eventually gave way to joy and trepidation. I am joyful because it has been half a year since the first term began at Nanyang University. I am delighted to note that everything has been progressing smoothly in an orderly manner. I have a sense of trepidation, for we have only just embarked on our journey and there is still a long way to go, with much yet to accomplish. I hope that the teachers will continue to nourish the students relentlessly and that students will study diligently and enjoy their learning everyday. The University is like a big family, with the teachers as the parents and the students, their children. Together, we will grow in width and depth each day, and steer towards the ultimate end of perfection. The going will be tough, and we must hold steadfastly to our purpose. The more effort we put in from within the University, the more support we will receive from the public. With more supporters, the foundation of our University will be consolidated, and we will be able to do things better; scale greater heights, expand our efforts and establish our reputation. This is a simple logic of cause and effect, and proportional reciprocation. Let us hope that all is well that ends well.

9.12 Speaking on the Student Movement Surrounding the Chinese High School and Chung Cheng High School

The Labour Front government of Singapore in September 1956 imposed measures against thousands of high school students participating in student movement on October 11, 1956. The Minister for Education Chew Swee Kee summoned the management board members of the Chinese High School and Chung Cheng High School to tell them to shut down the schools. The Ministry would arrange for teachers and students to continue their classes in some English schools.

The meeting agreed to issue a joint statement in reply to the Minister. In this reply the meeting informed the Minister that the boards could not be held responsible for executing the Ministry order to shut down the two high schools instead, the Ministry should be held responsible for any ensuing consequence. The following is the transcript of Tan Lark Sye's speech:

"The root cause of the protest in the two schools is in fact triggered by party politics, without in anyway relating to concern for local education. Although Chinese schools receive a token sum of government subsidy, which in effect are taxations derived from the Chinese community and therefore should not be of any big issue. The boards of Chinese schools all along came up with our own money to run the schools, so it is right for them to have a say in running of the schools independent of external interference. Even if the Government does not provide subsidy, we can still run the schools very well without the pittance from the government. Many of the directors present are not local citizens, so you are in fact grooming talents for this government. One thing we should understand, that we should not blindly obey every order from the government, but we should have our own visions. This crisis that has erupted in our two schools is actually resulting from the incompetence of the government in their handling, and not because of the Boards' ignorance.

On October 12 the same year, Tan Lark Sye spoke up again on this incident, in which he pointed out that the Minister of Education Chew Swee Kee's accusation of Tan Lark Sye's defense for the students was done for the sake of his own interests. Here is a transcript of Tan's rejoinder:

"I question Mr. Chew's ability to understand Chinese as he was ignorant of the minute resolutions of the previous boards' meeting and the adopted documents that he came up with distorted facts afterwards.

I have of late relatively paid less attention to the issue of Chinese education, even though I am still the Vice Chairman of the Board of the Chinese High School and President of the Hokkien Huay Kuan, reason being The Chinese High School board is in the good hands of its capable Chairman, while the five schools administered by the Hokkien Huay Kuan is under the purview of its Education Department. I do not need to concern myself with personnel matters. The reason I am speaking up now is simply because I was present at the joint board meeting of Chung Cheng High School and Chinese High Schools yesterday.

Mr. Chew alleged my statement at the previous meeting that "the root cause of the protest in Chung Cheng and Chinese High Schools is in fact related to party politics" was ridiculous. I find his perception of this matter to be utterly groundless. There has been ample evidence by way of radio broadcast, newspaper publication and government statements that many recent arrests in Singapore are overwhelmingly associated with a certain political party. I believe the millions of discerning residents would be able to see for themselves the root cause of it. Why then Mr. Chew has totally deviated from public opinion that sets him apart from the rest of the populace?

Mr. Chew's accusation that I am "defending the students to absolve them of all wrong-doings" is even more alarming. As an incumbent minister, Mr. Chew must be cautious of what he said. When have I ever defended the students and why should I? The messy state of Chinese schools today is all because of Mr. Chew's handling.

Mr. Chew's allegation that I spoke up "primarily for my own interests, while partly also for absolving the wrongs of subversive elements in Singapore" is malicious. I have lived here for over 40 years and during this time all that I have done are solely for the benefit of the local community and its people's welfare. As to how successful am I in this endeavour, I leave the verdict to the community. I can assure him by saying that all that I have said and done are not for my own interests. Let me pose this same question back to Mr. Chew: has he done anything that benefits the people prior to and during his term of office as Minister of Education? I am but a citizen with no party affiliation. All my efforts have been motivated by my enthusiasm to benefit the local government and the public. Since when have I defended the student activists, and why should I defend the subversive elements? I urge Minister Chew to exercise caution in his remarks and in particular to weigh on my rebuttal carefully before replying."

9.13 Seeking New Medications for the "Tuberculosis" of the Rubber Industry

As the president of Singapore Rubber Association, Tan Lark Sye led delegates from three rubber trade associations to attend the "Britain–Malaya Rubber Conference" held in London from May 27 to June 1, 1957, for the interests of the rubber manufacturers in Singapore and Malaya. On May 10, the three rubber associations held a send-off dinner for Tan Lark Sye at the Tanjong Rhu Club. The following is the speech delivered by Tan Lark Sye at the dinner.

I am honoured to be invited to this send-off dinner tonight by the three rubber associations. Present tonight are many of my fellow colleagues from the rubber industry, which goes to show how concerned we are over the common interests of the Chinese rubber traders. I am very excited by this display of solidarity.

The rubber conference that I am going to attend in Britain is held to resolve the issues of rubber exports from our Malaya federation and the arbitration of rubber prices, so as to find a good solution to the difficulties we face in rubber packing for export. Currently, we, the rubber exporters of Singapore and Malaya, are akin to have contracted "tuberculosis"; and we need to seek out new medications before the sickness deteriorates beyond cure.

Businessmen from Europe and Western countries came here with the intention of dominating the primary exporters' market here in Singapore and Malaya, squeezing out local businesses like us to contend with the secondary exporters' market. This stranglehold was established both before and after the war. They always got all the primary export deals.

Over these past decades, I had fought against the monopoly of the rubber market by the Western businesses when I was the president of the Rubber Association. Back in 1953, when I stepped down as president of Rubber Association, the Legislative Assembly passed the Rubber Packing, Distribution and Export Act, and set up the Rubber Export Registration Bureau. These actions by the authorities served to facilitate the Western businessmen to dominate the rubber exports market and to exclude us locals from benefitting from the rubber business. With the government behind them, the Western businesses controlled all the rights and the interests of the industry. At the same time, the government passed a corresponding law, stating that if any local businessmen delivered goods that were not complying to agreement, they would either have their licenses revoked or be fined 25,000 dollars or be given a three-years' imprisonment. This is a terrible blow to our local businesses.

However, in the three to four years since the Act went into effect, the government had yet to neither revoke the licenses of any local business nor imprison anyone, except for fining some of a few thousands of dollars. This had proved that the Export Monopoly Act was not workable and did not benefit the locals. They also knew that things were different now that Singapore was going to become independent, unlike the time when we were easy meat under the colonial rule. The policies from then are obsolete today and need to be revised.

I'd like to point out that in the past three to four years, local businessmen had been spared from having their licenses revoked or from imprisonment. Thanks to Mr. Chan Pui Hei, who had been fighting for the interests of the local industry. We had all benefitted from his hard work that was carried out in line with the aim of this association.

The Malayan Rubber Export Registration Bureau was like shackles put on the local people. Its existence costs hundreds of thousands of dollars every year, paid for by the local people. Yet, it never spoke on behalf of the local businesses when our prices were unjustly slashed. Before the bureau was set up, businessmen from the United States came over to buy up between thirty and forty thousand tons of rubber; but now, American orders had drastically reduced and even the volume of rubber shipped by our manufacturers to the United States had dwindled. Adding injury to insult is the fact that America is now buying rubber from Siam and Indonesia instead. In the past, it was rare for our European trading partners to slash our prices. After the bureau was set up, our prices were always slashed on our shipment to them. They would slash two or three pence for every pound of rubber, equivalent to an enforced discount of around twenty percents. They had the audacity to do this because our country had been placed at a disadvantage — (the overseas buyers can complain while the local businesses are hampered by the Act). Some of us had to resort to begging our buyers behind closed door for a smaller price cut, for fear of imprisonment and fines. As a result, not only did rubber businesses find it hard to earn a profit, they were even eating into capital. That is why I say the local rubber industry has developed "tuberculosis".

In the past, our rubber industry was reputed in the international market and many buyers from other countries came to Singapore to conduct business with us. Unfortunately, the government adopted the Act in the name of protecting our reputation, demanding that we delivered only good-quality rubber. The fact was, we were accused of fraud even when we delivered Grade A rubber to buyers who ordered Grade D rubber and we were unfairly handed down a price penalty. This is a stark contrast to the practice in Indonesia, where their government prohibits the export of good-quality rubber. For years many businessmen were thrown into prison in Indonesia and they had yet to be released. It was thus clear that businesses needed to come up with ingenious ways to deal with the governments to earn some money.

Last year, when the Singapore–Malaya Business Trade delegates visited China, they did not suffer price slash in the hands of China when nearly ten thousand tons of rubber were transacted. Yet when we traded with Europe, price cuts were always imposed, reason being the local Western businesses were conspiring with their European counterparts to usurp the interest of the local people. I knew very well that for each pound of rubber, the price cut was at least twenty percent. The setup of the Malayan Rubber Export Registration Bureau had not been beneficial to us locals but provoked a widespread discontent among traders. It is for this reason that I dare to accuse the bureau for conspiring with the Europeans.

If this bureau continues to operate, the fate of our colleagues is bleak. I have been honoured to be the president of the Rubber Association for over twenty years, and I am deeply troubled by the prospect that despite our current membership of over a hundred companies, someday this association may be left without any member. I am making this trip to see how they are going to suck our blood. As to whether this bureau will remain, it is up to the government, far beyond my capacity. I also feel that, upon my return, we should convene a general meeting to review the association's charter, to keep up with the changing times. We should make it a law that the presidency of our association should not be held by anyone for more than two terms. In closing, I thank you again for your kind gesture and support tonight. We will try our best to find a "new medication" on our return.

9.14 The Inauguration Ceremony of Nanyang University

Nanyang University held a grand inauguration ceremony on March 30, 1958, with a hundred thousand people turning up to witness the occasion. Such a level of participation was unparalleled in the history of Singapore. The following is the speech delivered by Tan Lark Sye at the ceremony.

Your Excellency, Honourable Members and Officials of the Government of Singapore and the Federation of Malaya, Ladies and Gentlemen:

Today we celebrate the completion of the first phase of our University's building programme. We are most grateful to His Excellency, the Governor Sir William Goode, representatives of the Federal and Singapore Governments and other honoured guests, some of whom have come a long way to attend this inauguration and their presence is a great honour to us.

I recall 1953 when I first mooted the establishment of this University, it was Sir William Goode, then Colonial Secretary, who was the first to support the idea with enthusiasm. On reading about it in the papers, Sir William Goode invited me to see him. In the ensuing interview, Sir Goode said many an encouraging word and expressed the hope that the proposed University would not take long to materialise. He also promised that he would facilitate matters with regard to registration of the University, its site and other problems attendant upon the founding of the University. This generous support from Sir Goode has made it possible for these imposing structures of the first phase of our University's building programme to rise amid the scenic landscape of the Yunnan Park; for the University's academic programme to be carried through according to plan and for students coming from various parts of South East Asia, in swelling numbers from year to year, to enter into the third year of their academic career. It has been plain sailing from the beginning. That is why I say we owe first of all to Sir Goode for the success of this University, and for that reason there is no one more suitable for officiating in today's ceremony than his Excellency. I am sure Sir Goode's joy on this occasion must be greater than ours.

The objectives of our University have been made public from time to time. Briefly, they are to provide this country's need for high-grade trained personnels in various fields; to promote an interflow of the different cultures domiciled in Malaya, thereby building racial harmony and cooperation. From this interflow of the diverse cultures in our midst, we hope in due course a new culture of South East Asia will rise, with Malaya and Singapore as its cradle, which will contribute to progress and peace of the world. I believe this hope is not only shared by all those who are present but by all peoples of South East Asia as well.

Though the Nanyang University is modelled somewhat on the well known universities in China, our medium of instruction is in fact bilingual, equal importance being placed on Chinese and English. Plans are in hand to set up Malay and Indian studies. There are two aspects to any branch of learning; the theoretical and the practical. Where the theoretical aspect is concerned, we aim to keep abreast of the foremost institutes of learning in the world and together with them strive towards a perfect academic environment notwithstanding it is an endless endeavour. As to the practical aspect, it is our concern to meet the needs of the time and place. Nanyang University has come into being in a period of history characterised by amazing speed in scientific progress and also in a location where people of diverse racial origins have lived and worked for generations. To infuse an enthusiasm for the science into our University life is therefore an urgent task and to undertake studies of several cultures domiciled in Malaya and the teaching of their respective languages is however regarded as primary objectives of the University. For one to be monolingual in English is to confine oneself to a much smaller world in the context of South East Asia. However, in the world, it is to shut oneself from half of it. To know Chinese and English but without a knowledge of Malay and

Indian will also prove inadequate in the Singapore and Malaya of tomorrow. It is on this conviction that the educational programs of this University are formulated so that we are not oblivious of the needs of our time and place, nor the importance of the study of theory and practice. That is why I have always made bold announcement to the world that Nanyang University is a truly national university of Malaya and Singapore. Our graduates will no doubt be the kind of talents best suited for its varied purposes and find in excellent opportunities in South East Asia which will be the envy of graduates of other universities. Even in the context of the world at large the adaptability of our graduates will be unrivalled. That is my unshakeable belief.

Although Nanyang is founded by the Chinese community, it is not intended to keep it as such for the Chinese alone. On the contrary, it is intended to be shared by all brother communities domiciled here for generations. Nanyang's door is ever open to youths of all races who seek to pursue learning and knowledge. Proof of our sincerity is seen in an amendment to our admission rules and regulations. Under the amended rules, the requirement for the Chinese language has been lowered to a mere working knowledge of the spoken language (Kuoyu). To put into perspective, Nanyang University is a supreme gift presented to Singapore and Federation of Malaya by the Chinese over and above the taxation contributions. In doing so, we lighten the two governments' burden in providing higher education for their citizens so that they are capable of participating in the great task of nation building. In saying that, however, we do not forget the generous moral and material support this University has received from other communities.

More than 80% of our students are citizens of either Singapore or the Federation of Malaya. The rest have come from other parts of South East Asia, viz. Siam, Indonesia, Vietnam, the Philippines, Sarawak and Hong Kong. We expect future students will come from remoter parts of the world. We want to see every one of our students well-disciplined, law-abiding, industrious, loyal to the University, be generally good students and good members of our society. We want to see every one of our students going out into the world to be of

service to the countries of their domicile, to excel in their profes-
sions and to benefit society in general. That is why in their student
days, they are not allowed to take part in political activities, though
political studies are not excluded from our University. We also do
not allow our students to get involved in other uncalled for activities
of society. We well understand that an educational institution such
as this University has its dignity to safeguard while infiltration of
political parties into schools, due to short-sightedness of party politicians, will undermine in its strive for academic excellence. The
failure of a school is the failure of its students which in turn brings
failure to society and the state. If society and the state are under-
mined in the process, how could party politicians escape a similar
fate? Being aware of this danger we have made it clear time and
again that our University is an educational institution, pure and
simple, and is only concerned with the advancement of learning. It
is free from any political tint and uncommitted to the support of any
political party. It is also clearly spelt out in our staff employment
contract that staff should observe this principle both in word and
in deed.

Since its establishment two years ago, our University has built up
a good tradition visible to the public. During the unrest in October
1956, it is noted that many schools were closed for many days, the
University carried on with lectures and classes as usual — without
interruption. This is proof that our teachers and students are of one
mind in fostering the tradition of the University and in displaying
their care and love for the University and the country. This glorious
example should be encouraged and perpetuated as a model to all
the other schools.

The fifth session of the Representatives of the Regional
Committees of the University has approved a draft Nanyang
University Ordinance submitted by our lawyers. When the Ordinance
is passed by the Legislative Assembly, it will become the permanent
charter of the University. The central organisation will be the
University Council which is made up of Representatives of the
Regional Committee; faculty members; guild of graduates and of
the government. This organisation shall combine the wisdom of the

University administration, the boards of directors, faculty and students to run the University. This organisation shall also bring together the Government and the people for an open and coordinated partnership. This, we declare, will be our unique spirit and solid foundation on which to fulfil our mission.

The donations pledged and collected will be published in the papers from time to time. We solicit for funds: we collect them and we build and we construct according to our plans. We never dare to ease up. Our University endeavours to manage the funds with prudence so that we will not overspend indiscriminately otherwise we would not have been able to present the University before you today. Can we say that our University has sufficient funds? No, we say that in this respect it is far from ideal. Funding for this undertaking has no limit, and it is particularly so in higher education. The more the funding the better it will be. Then, are our funds inadequate? If people would be liberal and give generously, who knows that the University funds in the future would not be more adequate than it is now.

On this auspicious occasion, I myself most humbly and respectfully offer the University this wish: though the drums of celebration may last for a day, the music of education will be sung for ages.

9.15 May Teachers Be Dedicated Persons of Noble Cause With Ideals, and Students Energetic as Lions and Dragons

After the inauguration ceremony of Nanyang University on March 30, 1958, Tan Lark Sye, as president of the University, published a written statement to express his gratitude towards the public and the 100,000-strong turnout at the ceremony for their support, to list the financial needs of the University with the increase in student intake, and to encourage the faculty and students to work hard to bring honour to Nanyang University.

On behalf of Nanyang University, I hereby extend my deepest gratitude to the Guest-of-Honour, Sir William Goode, and all the government officials, consuls from various embassies, and guests from various ethnic groups for gracing the University's inauguration ceremony. I would also like to thank all the individuals and institutions for your well-wishes, gifts and for extending to us outfits and personnel.

I would like to apologise for the paralysed traffic along the whole stretch of Jurong Road due to overwhelming number of visitors and their vehicles. Although this was a strong sign of support from the people, it also showed a lapse on our part in our preparation for the event. For this, I offer my deepest apology.

Despite the University only at the initial stage, our criteria for admitting students are rigorous. We planned for 1,200 current and new students this year, but the number of applicants has already reached this number, and we had to turn away over 700 of them. The total number of new and current students has already exceeded 1,300 since registration started, including those who passed the entrance examination last year but deferred their admission for a year. At present, we have barely enough classrooms and faculty dormitories. We are facing a severe shortfall of student dormitory space, for over 30 girls and over 80 boys are unable to find on-campus accommodation. We also regret that we had to say no to the daily deluge of letters from those who wish to attend audition classes. To these students, I am most sympathetic and regretful.

Next year we will enter our fourth academic year. How, then, can we not increase our enrollment? With more students, we would have to expand our faculty strength. Based on the current trend, more parents desire to send their children for tertiary education, and more graduates from both Chinese and English high schools wish to further their studies. We estimate that if we increase our enrollment by 600, the University will need to come up with $5,000 for every new student to cover the cost of building and equipping more classrooms and dormitories for students and faculty. That means the total cost to house the additional 600 students will come up to $3 million, and that does not include the additional costs for library books and equipments. However, our University has about $1.6 million in our account now. Including the estimated $700,000 in gifts received during this inauguration ceremony, the University's fund stands at $2.4 million. Even if we deplete our finances to meet the cost of completing three portions of the expansion next year, there will still be a deficit of between $700,000 to $800,000. Although the construction cost of the second building for the Science Faculty is about $300,000, the total cost of building and equipping the new building will come up to $1 million, based on the experience of setting up the first Science Faculty building. So far, we have only talked about the construction costs. How about the fund for monthly expenditures?

The scale of this inauguration ceremony is unprecedented in the history of Singapore, which is something to rejoice about. However, after a moment of contemplation, I am filled with trepidation! How can we repay the staunch support that the society has showered us with? How shall we deliver our duties so that this University will grow from strength to strength?

A good government does not speak irresponsibly, just as a good leader of a political party does not make empty promises. The stream of sympathy and praise from the government and various political parties have been pouring in steadily, for which we are very grateful and encouraged! However, in the University's quest to be encompassing, meticulous and lasting, we need to rely on our determination and self-reliance. The Chinese community in the South Sea (Nanyang) region has a good tradition of public spiritedness and zealousness for the common good. Once we commence an undertaking, we will see it to completion. Some will take the role of fore runners, while others will carry it forth. Therefore, those who have yet to fulfill their pledges of donations will surely honour them eventually. The delegates from the various University committees all over the region will eventually keep their promise of campaigning for more funds. We have complete faith in them and we thank them for their support! When I think this, my trepidation seems unwarranted.

Rumour has it that the University of Malaya will be officially divided into two campuses: one will remain at its original premises in Singapore, and the other will be in Kuala Lumpur. We hope that the University of Malaya in Kuala Lumpur will follow the lead of its sister campus in Singapore's to set up a Chinese Department to meet the actual needs of society. We are confident that, with the guidance of the authorities and the financial support from taxpayers' money, the Chinese Departments of the University of Malaya in Singapore and Kuala Lumpur will provide quality college education for Chinese high school graduates, so that the mounting enrollment pressure placed on Nanyang University can be relieved.

Now, I would like to say a few words to the faculty.

Most of you have come from afar to work here in response to your calling to the noble mission of education. If not for your passion for the education cause, and the sense of responsibility that you placed upon yourselves, why would you have braved all the difficulties to join us here? The University may not have sufficiently accorded you the honour that you deserve, yet we are sincere and earnest in our dealings with you. We have no doubt that you, sirs, are dedicated educators who can help write a new chapter in the history of our relatively-backward Nanyang culture. Your names will be glorious and everlasting as the cause that you are now a part of. The University needs many people with different academic degrees — bachelors, masters, doctorates — to work as teaching assistants, lecturers, associate professors and professors. Yet the qualification that we need most urgently are people with the highest honorary degree, and these are "persons who dedicate themselves to a noble cause". It is easy to find learned men, but dedicated people to noble cause are hard to come by. This title cannot be conferred by others, but is taken upon by oneself. Once taken upon by oneself, one will live in a manner worthy of the title. I hope that everyone of our University faculty — regardless of your academic qualifications — bachelor, master, doctorate, non-bachelor, non-master, non-doctorate — are all dedicated people.

And now, I would like to address our students in our University:

You are aware of the difficulties to pursue higher education, but do you know also the difficulties of running a University? Nanyang University exists only with the money and hard work contributed by many people in our population, and after overcoming innumerable obstacles and setbacks. For Nanyang University to survive and grow, a large number of people will need to continuously donate for the cause. Without Nanyang University, many of you would have only a secondary education. You should therefore count yourself fortunate. Now that Nanyang University is founded, it must be run well, which means it must at least be a university living up to its name. For a university to be recognised as a reputable institution, much depends upon its academic excellence. Therefore, the primary task for the chancellor, deans and department heads lie in the search and recruitment of good teachers. The better teachers they engage, the more competent they are at their job. A good university is one that excels academically. This will be the guideline for our University in all our future undertaking. The attendance by a hundred thousand guests at this inauguration ceremony bears witness to two things: first, the irrefutable existence of Nanyang University; second, Nanyang University has mass support of the people, and it belongs to the people. Henceforth, if the people fail to support the University, the people would have failed you; conversely, if you fail to study hard, you would have failed the people. My dearest students! Remember the expectations of your parents, the community and the country! If you do not forge ahead of the relentless time and tide, you will be left behind! The flag hoisted at the inauguration ceremony will serve to guide you; the stirring drums and gongs at the ceremony serve to encourage you! Like the prancing lions and soaring dragons at the ceremony, you should pursue your studies with as much vigour and enthusiasm! The name of this University is now part of you; and your names in aggregate will represent the name of this University. Henceforth, your fame or infamy, your success or failure, they are inseparable from this University!

9.16 In Defense of Nanyang University's Ten-Year Plan

The Nanyang University Assessment Panel, headed by Professor S. I. Prescott, vice-chancellor of University of Western Australia, was formed under the Labor Front government to assess the academic level of Nanyang University. It published a report in July 1959. On July 23 of the same year, Dr. Gwee Ah Leng, with a number of individuals, was appointed by the education minister of the People's Action Party government to a review committee tasked to assess the Prescott report. Later, the committee and the management committee of Nanyang University held a joint meeting to exchange opinions. The following is the speech delivered by Tan Lark Sye, president of Nanyang University Executive Committee at the meeting.

I agree with the points raised by Mr. Chairman. Earlier, I have already made a five-year and ten-year plan for the development of Nanyang University, with which Mr. Lien Shih Sheng and Mr. Liao Song Yang are familiar. In view of the harmonious atmosphere we have today, I'd like to bring them up again for your reference.

The aim of Nanyang University is to nurture talents for Singapore and Malaya. Back at the Conference of Chinese Associations in 1953, held to discuss matters of the Nanyang University, the two hundred-odd participants unanimously agreed to the need to establish Nanyang University. Since then, I have been sure and confident about the establishment of this university.

Objectives

We intended to establish a Chinese university similar to those well-known universities run by the Anglo-American churches in China, where equal emphasis is placed on Chinese and English. To adapt to the local conditions, we planned to offer Malay courses in 1957, which was officially realised the following year. Currently, apart from

Chinese and English, Nanyang University students have made good progresses in the learning Malay. Some students have even compiled and published a Malay dictionary. This demonstrated that Nanyang University is truly a people's university, for these three languages are most needed in Singapore and Malaya. In addition, students may choose to learn other languages like French and/or German according to their individual needs for the purpose of pursuing higher education overseas.

Chinese is the lingua franca for most Asians. It is estimated that the number of Chinese users all over the world has reached 800 million. English is the lingua franca of the Western hemisphere, i.e. Europe and the business community. Malay is the major language spoken in Singapore, Malaya, and Indonesia. Unlike graduates from other universities, the first cohort of Nanyang University graduates can speak more than one language. They will become the most versatile employees in any government departments and society in Singapore and Malaya. They will stand a greater advantage if they work in either Chinese, Malay and/or English newspapers.

Financial Problems

Now I'd like to talk about the financial difficulties of Nanyang University. Since 1953, Nanyang University has received pledges totaling about $20 million payable by installments over either 10 or 20 years, of which $13 million has been received. To date, the University's expenditure has exceeded $14 million. There are still $7 million of pledges outstanding for circumstantial reasons.

Last May or June, Mr. Richard Lim Chuan Hoe, then-Deputy Speaker of the Legislative Assembly, announced in the newspapers that he was moved by the achievements of Nanyang University and proposed that the government should provide $5 million in subsidies to our University. However, the funds received from the government amounted to only $385,000. Yet, the public has already been misled by the "news" of the government's intention to provide substantial funding to Nanyang University. As a result, donations dried up, and many who had made pledges earlier on stopped honouring their pledges. Nanyang University's finance has thus been greatly impaired.

Currently, Nanyang University's dormitories, classrooms and facilities can barely accommodate 2,000 students. Concerned that we have reached saturation, we have planned to construct a building on a fifty thousand square feet plot which houses an auditorium with a 5,000-seat capacity on the ground floor. Of the four levels over the auditorium, one level that covers over ten thousand square feet will be set apart for the University administration so as to free up the space that it occupies in the library at the moment. The rest of the building will be partitioned into new classrooms. In addition, we have planned to build a large sports stadium. The total cost estimated for the building and equipping of the auditorium and the stadium is $1.5 million, of which the auditorium would cost $700,000 and the stadium between $700,000 to $800,000. So far, only Hokkien Huay Kuan has committed to $600,000 for the construction of the auditorium, plus the $1 million in donation that we were expecting to receive this year, we were hopeful that these two projects will be completed smoothly. However due to the circumstance mentioned above, both major projects are shelved for this year.

Another Obstacle

Another man-made obstacle has to do with the incident last year, when the authorities conferred with the former chairman of the Nanyang University Administrative Committee and Dean of the Arts Faculty, Mr. Zhang Tianze, to put the University under an academic assessment by a panel. As far as I know, no university established in China so far has had such need for this so-called assessment panel. Accordingly, this concerns the recognition of the degrees issued by our University. In fact, I think it has nothing to do with the recognition of our degrees. Back then, I was strongly against the proposal because, to me, Nanyang University was like a healthy person who had no need for a doctor as it was not sick at all. I suspected that someone was intentionally poisoning our cause, as this development could either destroy or paralyse this University. It had turned out exactly as I have suspected. The release of the report from the assessment panel has put Nanyang University's future in jeopardy. This is the other man-made obstacle that I mentioned just now.

Nonetheless, our first phase plan to take in 2,000 students by 1960 has been achieved successfully.

Second Phase Plan

Now, I'd like to present a summary of the University's second phase plan. According to our plan, the University's second phase plan will commence in 1961, increasing our enrollment by 300 students each year; in other words, our student population will increase to 2,300 by 1961, 2,600 by 1962, and so on till 1965. For every additional student, the University will need $5,000 more for the building of dormitories, classrooms and other facilities. Based on the additional 300 students in 1961, we will need $1.5 million for the expansion of our facilities, plus another $500,000 for books and equipments. These two items would come up to $2 million. On top of this, the University still subsidise every student $1,000 every year. For the 2,300 students in 1961, total subsidies will amount to $2.3 million. Adding all these up, Nanyang University's expenditure in 1961 stands at $4.3 million, $4.6 million in 1962, and $5.5 million by 1965 when enrollment hits 3,500 students.

However, this was our original plan. Due to the above obstacles I have mentioned, there is no telling whether the second-phase plan will materialise although the first phase plan has been completed. For instance, our expansion plan for the coming year has already been put on hold. For now, we can only hope to carry out the two major construction projects for the auditorium and the sports stadium, and to keep our target of taking in 2,000 students next year.

Salary Raise

There is one issue that I would like to clarify. Nanyang University has been criticised for the low salary paid to our faculty, and this has caused our faculties to become demoralised. I would like to take this opportunity to explain that, when we founded this University, we have planned that the salaries of our professors, associate professors, lecturers and teaching assistants are pegged proportionately to the salary level of teachers in the local Chinese primary and secondary schools. At the same time, our professors received a pay rise of 10% in their second year of service, and a raise of 5% in their third year of service. Their salaries would have been raised to a decent level if we were to continue with this remuneration scheme. However, again due to the obstacles mentioned before, this schemed was suspended at their fourth year of service.

Many among you, gentlemen of the committee, graduated from secondary schools in China and are more familiar with the universities in China. You are therefore in a better position to make fair comparisons between Nanyang University and the other Chinese universities.

We are currently overwhelmed by the number of applicants from Singapore and Malaya seeking to enter our University. For example, well over 1,000 candidates applied to Nanyang University every year, of which our University can admit only 30%. It is our hope that the governments in Singapore and Malaya will set up another university like ours to meet the needs of our local students. Meanwhile, I would say that I have already done my best to promote education locally.

9.17 The First Graduation Ceremony of Nanyang University

Nanyang University held its first graduation ceremony on April 2, 1960, much to the exultation of everyone on campus. The following speech was delivered by Tan Lark Sye, chairman of the Nanyang University Executive Committee.

Today we hold the first graduation ceremony of this University. I am deeply honoured by the presence of our distinguished government officials, guests and parents!

Nanyang University was founded in 1953, and the first batch of undergraduates started its first term on March 15, 1956. Over the last four years of hard works, our first cohort of graduates from various faculties had finally completed their courses ready to step out into the society. This is the first batch of our graduates. Over these four years, we invested over $10 million in buildings, and over $2.5 million in books, equipments and other facilities, excluding the books donated. Our student population increased in number from above 500 in the first year, 900 in the second year, 1,300 in the third year to 1,700 in the fourth, without including 300 students enrolled in our pre-university classes.

In terms of continuous material and spiritual support from the people in Singapore and the Malayan federation, and the growing number of applicants, we are convinced that the establishment of this University has met the needs of our society and justified the principal objectives of its establishment.

From our performance over the last four years, it is gratifying to note that our teachers and students have both settled steadfastly into their respective places, without any disruption or hiccup. The University remained open even under the most precarious circumstances, and this is proof that the teachers, students and the administration are managing well, and they are collectively shaping an excellent school culture. As the saying goes, "The beginning is always the most difficult". Still which university in the world has encountered such obstacles and problems as ours? Which "start-up" university has ever developed as steadily and fast as ours? The public can bear witness that it is truly remarkable for what our young University to achieve thus far! A number of established universities in Britain and United States have granted direct admission to many of our graduates into their post-graduate programs. The Singaporean government has also recognised the academic degrees conferred by our University by recruiting our graduates into various government services. All these have proven that our graduates have received a quintessentially university-level training in their four years of discipline, and their academic achievements cannot be unjustly questioned.

We are fully aware of our University shortcomings in its systems and administration. The hearsay that has been circulating around are, more often than not, distortions, misrepresentations, exaggerations and even fabrications. It is universally true that no institution or system is perfect. Even renowned universities with a long history have their shortcomings pertinent to them currently. Our university will have its own set of problems when it is 100 years from now. The issue is not the presence of shortcomings, but whether we are prepared to face it to improve on it with the passage of time. Over the last four years, we have been making improvements all the time, otherwise we would not have made it today. If we have not continued to be vigilant, and have failed to adjust to suit the needs of the times and the social environment, we would have no tomorrow. Progress is an unending process. There is no shame in having shortcomings, only when we do not pursue progress.

To our graduands: you are now university graduates. Today, Nanyang University will award you your graduate's qualification and diploma. To you, this is an honour; yet, on the other hand, it is also your responsibility to the society, to the country and to all mankind. The end of a stage in your life signals the beginning of a new one. No matter what jobs you may engage in after you graduate — be it manufacturing, business, agriculture, education or any other vocations, or continue with academic research, you must apply what you have learnt and work hard to realise your aspirations and achieve your dreams. We live and learn unrelentingly. There are still so many things waiting for you to discover in your work. Human beings are political creatures, so you can of course join any political party according to your own conviction. Simply put, I only have two pieces of advice for you: the first one is "Be Loyal to Your Country" and the second one is "Bring The Greatest Happiness to the Most Number of People". I remember reminding all the students at the inauguration ceremony held two years ago, "The name of this University is now part of yours; and your names will collectively represent the name of this University. Henceforth, your glory or dishonour, your success or failure, they are inseparable from this University!" Today, I would like to offer my congratulations to you and your parents on this note.

Having the first batch of graduates, we will see the second, the third and many future batches of graduates, streaming out of university. Nanyang University is founded by the people and belongs to the people in Singapore and Malaya. Therefore the critical guidelines of our University must also be endorsed by the people in Singapore and Malaya. Nanyang University is truly a public university owned by the people in Singapore and Malaya. If the people wish the University to be alive forever, it will be so. On this happy occasion, allow me to offer my most heartfelt wishes to our Nanyang University.

9.18 Performance and Expectation of Nanyang University Graduates

Nanyang University held its second graduation ceremony on March 3, 1961. As chairman of the Nanyang University Executive Committee, Tan Lark Sye offered his encouragement to the graduates in the following address.

Honourable Government officials, distinguished Guests, Parents, and representatives of the various Nanyang University committees, the faculty and students,

Today our University marks its second graduation ceremony. On behalf of the University, I would like to express my gratification to all present, and extend my congratulations in particular to our graduating students and their parents.

By now, a total of nearly 800 men and women from the University's first and second cohorts have graduated. They have started serving the society, be it in academic, political, industrial or commercial fields. The high employment rate of our graduates is truly heartening. Have they received the same level of training as provided by other universities in the world during their four years of study here? Have they found themselves academically and professionally fit to meet the needs in Singapore and Malaya? What you see here today is a forceful evidence.

Furthermore, we are also excited by the number of graduates pursuing higher degrees in universities in Europe, North America, Australia, New Zealand and other countries. Many among them are on scholarships and some have done us proud with their outstanding achievements. So, is the academic level of Nanyang University on par with most universities in the world? Have the universities in Europe, North America, Australia and New Zealand and other countries recognised the academic qualification conferred by Nanyang University? Here, again, provide another forceful evidence.

The faculties and departments in Nanyang University have been set up with certain objectives in mind, it seeks to serve the nation loyally and stays true to our Malayan culture. This is why I declare yet again, that Nanyang University is a people's university for Singapore and Malaya. The Chinese, English and Malay languages can be likened to the cultural soil of Singapore and Malaya; and Nanyang University is toiling over this cultural soil of our two countries which are fertilised by the equatorial rainfall and sunshine. This is why we can only yield durians and rambutans but not lychees and longans.

There will be an increasing number of graduates streaming out from Nanyang University; hopefully, their level of academic achievements will also be higher and higher. Your achievements in your careers will depend on your hard work after your graduation. I would like to take this opportunity today to offer a few words of encouragement as my parting gift for you:

Aspire to benefit the people. Be loyal, brave and modest. Always forge ahead in your studies and career.

You are the new blood of the society, the driving force of our country. You should dedicate your youthful energy to serve the society and the country, so that this society and this country can benefit from your dedication. Thanks to you, when society progresses, it brings glory to the people; when a nation progresses, it makes the people proud. This glory and pride will belong to you, your parents and Nanyang University.

The existence of Nanyang University has been justified by the society's acceptance and the recognition of various oversea universities. Without a doubt, Nanyang University must and will continue to make its presence felt. Nanyang University was founded by the people, and thus will always be supported by the people. However, to sustain the growth of the sacred mission of Nanyang University will much depend on tripartite understanding and cooperation of the Board of Directors, faculty and students. At the same time, our University should constantly evaluate and reflect on ourselves, and accept constructive suggestions from people outside the University.

Over the years, we have overcome difficulties of various shades and sizes for Nanyang University to make as much achievements as it did today. At the threshold of 1961, let us be of one mind, one conviction; let us persist in our endeavour to ensure Nanyang University progresses relentlessly towards a future without any perimeter.

Profile of the Contributors

Pan Guo Qu (Pan Shou)	Former secretary general of Nanyang University. Poet and Calligrapher.
Lim Hoon Yong	From the pioneer batch of graduates from the Department of Economics and Politics, Nanyang University. He was awarded Public Administration Medal (Gold) in 1977.
Ong Chu Meng	From the pioneer batch of graduates from the Department of Economics and Politics, Nanyang University.
Choi Kwai Keong	From the pioneer batch of graduates from the Department of History and Geography, Nanyang University. Researcher, Institute of Overseas Chinese Studies.
Koay How Khim	From the 2nd batch of graduates from the Department of History and Geography, Nanyang University.
Lim How Seng	From the 7th batch of graduates from the Department of History, Nanyang University.

Au Yue Pak	From the 5th batch of graduates from the Department of Chinese language and Literature, Nanyang University.
	Journalist.
Ng Kim Eng	From the 2nd batch of graduates from the Department of History and Geography, Nanyang University.
	Freelance writer.
Tan Yam Seng	From the pioneer batch of graduates from the Department of Economics and Politics, Nanyang University.
Ng Lai Yang	Engineer MISE; Ph.D in Political Science, Kansas State University.
Siw Ming Wei	Freelance Writer.

Editor's Note

Lim Hoon Yong
Editor

Articles in this English transcript are all contributed by Nanyang University alumni except for the one by Pan Shou (ex-secretary general NU). These articles were written originally in Chinese language.

Generally, the articles relate to the writers' passions for founding of the University: their lives in the campus during the times of uncertainty and the tribute they paid unanimously to the founder of their alma mater.

However, the mood and mode of expression permeates the cries for the University, the alumni and the undergraduates in their struggle for recognition of their academic degrees and appropriate positioning of the University within the Nation's education framework.

Members of the Editorial Board are aware of their pursuits and expectations. However, the Editorial Board follows rigidly a guiding discipline in translation works, i.e., to stay close to the writer's aspiration and be honest to their text. In our effort to keep to this discipline, we have to compromise between the mood of the texts and smooth reading of the English transcript. Furthermore some repetition of themes and substances appearing before us in some articles (although by different writers) are also unavoidable.

Finally we appeal to our readers to bear with us on the translation works, particularly in this case where the Chinese and the English are totally of different language structure. We therefore apologise for any inconveniences caused.

Glossary

Aihua Music Society 爱华音乐社
Aik Hoe Rubber Company 益和树胶公司
Allied 联盟
Ang Chye Chuan 洪再泉
Asia Insurance Company Ltd 亚洲保险有限公司
Asia Life Insurance Company Ltd 亚洲人寿保险有限公司
Atlantic Charter 大西洋宪章
Au Yue Pak 区如柏
Autumn Harvest Uprising 秋收起义
Aw Boon Chuan 胡文钏
Aw Boon Haw 胡文虎
B. R. Sreenivasan 史林尼哇山
Bank of See Teong Wah 四海通銀行
Beijing 北京
Boon Choo 文知
Book Without Words 无字天书
Boon Tat 文达
British commander Arthur Percival 英军司令白思华
Chan Mee Leen 陈美莲
Chang Ming Thien 张明添
Chang Weilong 陈维龙
Chen Hua Mu 陈华木
Chen Shujuan 陈淑娟
Chen Yanlin 陈炎林
Chen Zhong Nan 陈宗南
Cheng Yuling 陈毓灵
Cheong Kim Nan 张金鸾
Cheong Soon Chou 张顺畴

Chew Swee Kee 周瑞麒
Chia Hsing 嘉兴
Chiang Kai-Shek 蒋介石
Chief Minister David Marshall 首席部长马绍尔
Chinese Chamber of Commerce 中华总商会
Chinese United League 同盟会
Chong Fu Primary School 崇福学校
Choi Kwai Keong 崔贵强
Chong Hock Girl School 崇福学校
Chong Mong Sang 張梦生
Choong Sam 钟森
Chua Siew Ching 蔡秀琴
Chuan Deng 传灯
Chui Huai Lim 醉花林
Chung Hua Hua Nan School 中华化南学校
David Gwilym James 詹姆斯
Dong Lixi 董黎熙
Dr. C. F. Young 杨进发博士
Dr. Chuang Chu Lin 庄竹林博士
Dr. Gwee Ah Leng 魏雅聆医生
Dr. Han Suyin 韩素英医生
Dr. Lee Zhao Ming 李昭铭博士
Dr. Pan Siying 潘思颖医生
Dr. Rayson Huang Lisung 黄丽松博士
Dr. Xiong Shulong 熊叔隆博士
Ee Hoe Hean Club 怡和轩俱乐部
Emperor Guangxu 光绪皇帝
Empress Dowager Cixi 慈禧太后
Eng Bo 永博
Eng Chin 永进
Eng Ghee 永义
Eng Han 永汉
Eng Ho 永和
Eng Keong 永琼
Eng Sen 永森
Eng Seng 永生

Eng Shun 永顺
Eng Sin 永新
Eng Wah 永华
Eng Yi 永义
Five Treaty Ports 五口通商港
Foo Chee Fong 符致逢
Foo Yet Kai 胡曰皆
Fuzhou 福州
Gan Eng Seng School 颜永成学校
Gan Kok Koon 颜国钧
Gao Dunhou 高敦厚
George E. Lee 李玉荣
Goh Chye Hin 吴再兴
Goh Keng Swee 吴庆瑞
Goh Swee Khim 伍瑞琴
Great World Amusement Park 大世遊艺场
Guo Shanhu 郭珊瑚
Hakka 客家
He Hua 何华
Ho Wing Shun 何永信
Hokkien Association 福建会馆
Hong Changshu 洪長树
Hong Qidu 洪啓读
Hong Yong An (Hong Yong'an) 洪永安
Hu Boyuan 胡博渊
Hu shi 胡适
Hu Zizhou 胡资周
Huang Di 黄帝
Huang Fukang 黄復康
Huang Xiaoyun 黄啸云
Huang Zhuoshan 黄卓善
Jacen Hsieh 谢哲声
Jimmy Low 刘济琛
Joint Petition of Imperial Examination 公车上书
Kan Ah Suo 高亚思
Kang Kek Bu (Jiang Ke Wu) 江克武

Kang Youwei 康有为
Kedah 吉打
Ko Dow 科斗
Khua Chin Lai 柯进耒
Kim Chuan Road Rubber Factory 金泉律胶厂
Ko Teck Kin 高德根
Koay How Khim 郭孝谦
Koh Tin Kok 许镇国
Kong Chien School 光前学校
Kong Hwa School 光华学校
Kuah Chin Lai 柯进来
Lian Hoe Rubber Shop 联合树胶店
Lam Kwok Yan 林国仁
Lan Ying 兰英
Lan Yunzang 蓝允藏
Lao Liu 老六
Lau Geok Swee (Lin Yu Shui) 刘玉水
Lau Pa Sat 老巴刹
Lau Tai San 刘泰山
Lee Chin Tian 李振殿
Lee Kam Yoon 李金源
Lee Kim Chuan 李金泉
Lee Kong Chian 李光前
Lee Kuan Yew 李光耀
Lee Leung Ki 李亮琪
Lee Siow Mong 李紹茂
Legislative Assembly 立法议会
Lek Kim Koon 陆锦坤
Leng Kee Hill 麟记山
Li Dongfang 黎东方
Li Guochang 黎国昌
Li Liang Qi (Lee Leung Ki) 李亮琪
Li Ming 黎明
Li Po Wen 黎博文
Liang Qichao 梁启超
Lien Shih Sheng 连士升

Lien Ying Chow 连瀛洲
Lim Boh Seng 林谋盛
Lim Hoon Yong 林云扬
Lim How Seng 林孝胜
Lim Keng Nian (Lian) 林庆年
Lim Lian Gek (Lim Lian Geok) 林连玉
Lim Nee Soon 林义顺
Lim Shuqin 林叔欽
Lim Soon Tiong 林顺忠
Lim Yew Hock 林有福
Lin Fanglan 林芳兰
Lin Guorong 林国荣
Lin Juren 林居仁
Lin Taiyi 林太乙
Lin Yu Tang 林语堂
Linde Constitution Committee 林德宪制委员会
Luo Qingquan 骆清泉
Luo Xisheng 罗喜生
Malcolm MacDonald 麦唐纳
Mao Zedong 毛泽东
May Fourth Movement 五四运动
Mei Yiqi 梅贻琦
Merdeka 默迪卡
Nanjing 南京
Nanyang Culture Press 南洋文化出版社
Nego Soo Kee 吴师逮
New Era College 新纪元学院
Ng Aik Huan 黄奕欢
Ng Kim Eng 黄金英
Ng Lai Yang 吴乃炎
Ng Quee Lam (Huang Guinan) 黄桂楠
Ng Siew Kim 黄秀琴
Ng Soh Beng 黄叔明
Ng Tai Chun 黄大椿
Ng Toh San 黄卓善
Northern Warlords 北方军阀

Su Xiaoxian 苏孝先

Sun Yat-sen 孫中山

Ta Yu 大裕

Tan Boon Kat (Kue) 陈文确

Tan Cheng Lock 陈祯禄

Tan Chin Tuan 陈振传

Tan Chyi Guek 陈期岳

Tan Ee Leong 陈維龙

Tan Eng Ghee 陈永义

Tan Eng Joo 陈永裕

Tan Eng Kheng (Chin) 陈永进

Tan Eng Wah 陈永华

Tan Kah Kee 陈嘉庚

Tan Kee Peck 陈缨麟

Tan Keong Choon 陈共存

Tan Kin Hian 陈敬贤

Tan Kin Hian 陈敬贤

Tan Kong Piat 陈光别

Tan Lark Sye 陈六使

Tan Puay Chui 陈培水

Tan Shu Nan 陈树楠

Tan Siak Kew 陈锡九

Tan Sitong 谭嗣同

Tan Tong Nam 陈宗南

Tan Yam Seng 陈炎成

Tao Xingzhi 陶行知

Tay Koh Yat 郑古悦

Telok Ayer 直落亚逸

Teng Mah Seng 丁马成

The Eight Power Allied Force 八国联军

The Malaya Rubber Board 马来亚树胶出口注册局

The Twenty-one Demand 二十一条约

Three Peoples Doctrine 三民主义

Ting Beng Chin 丁明正

Tunku Abdul Rahman 东姑阿都拉曼

Ungku Abdul Aziz 翁姑阿芝

Viscount Alan Lennox-Boyd, Secretary of State for the Colonies
　殖民地大臣波德氏　(殖民部大臣林诺鲍)
Wang Shi Xiong (Wang Shixiong) 王世熊
Wang Zengbing 王增炳
Wei Yu Hui 魏毓辉
Wen Qin 文寝
Wen Que 文确
Wen Yi 文倚
Wen Zhang 文章
Wing On Fire Insurance Company 永安保险公司
Woo Mon Chew 胡文钊
World Youth Congress 世界青年大会
Wu Duxian 吴德贤
Wu Qiyuan 伍启元
Xinghua 兴化
Xiong Shiyi 熊式一
Xiu Ying 秀英
Yam Siew Khim 严秀钦
Yan Wenyu 严文郁
Yang Jiemei 杨介眉
Yang Shin Hua (Yang Xinghua) 杨惺华
Yang Zheng School 养正学校
Yap Phoeng Gek 叶平玉
Ye Fangfeng 叶帆风
Ye Yijian 叶怡煎
Yeo Chan Boon 杨缵文
Ying Xing 易行
Yong Chun 永春
Yong Nyuk Lin 杨玉麟
Yu Gang 余纲
Yuan Shikai 袁世凯
Zeng Xin Ying 曾心影
Zeng Zexing 曾则兴
Zhang Hansan 張汉三
Zhang Shu 張述
Zhang Tianze 張天泽

Zhang Weixuan 張緯軒
Zhang Xueliang 张学良
Zhang Ziqiu 张子秋
Zhangzhou 漳州
Zheng Kaiguo 郑开国
Zhou Jincai 周晋材
Zhou Xianrui 周献瑞